MIX
Papier aus verantwortungsvollen Quellen
Paper from responsible sources
FSC® C105338
FSC
www.fsc.org

Bernhard Stellner

Readability of Quarterly Reports

Do companies mislead investors?

Anchor Academic
Publishing

Stellner, Bernhard: Readability of Quarterly Reports. Do companies mislead investors?, Hamburg, Anchor Academic Publishing 2013

Buch-ISBN: 978-3-95489-148-1
PDF-eBook-ISBN: 978-3-95489-648-6
Druck/Herstellung: Anchor Academic Publishing, Hamburg, 2013

Bibliografische Information der Deutschen Nationalbibliothek:
Die Deutsche Nationalbibliothek verzeichnet diese Publikation in der Deutschen Nationalbibliografie; detaillierte bibliografische Daten sind im Internet über http://dnb.d-nb.de abrufbar.

Hermannstal 119k, 22119 Hamburg
http://www.diplomica-verlag.de, Hamburg 2013
Printed in Germany

Table of Content

List of Figures

List of Tables

1. Introduction

1.1 Aim of this Work

Financial reports can be regarded as the primary means of communication between a company's management and its shareholders. The reports also address all other kinds of stakeholders like employees, suppliers, customers, competitors, governments, potential investors, bond holders and, in a broad sense, the entire society.[1] Generally speaking, financial reports concern *"any group or individual who can affect or is affected by the achievement of the organization's objectives."*[2]

The reports aim to keep stakeholders informed about the business history, financial status and future expectations.[3] Typically, both narrative information and quantitative data are provided in firms' reports through the inclusion of financial statements, notes, discussion of operations and letters to the shareholders.[4] Investors to a great extent base their risk assessment and investment decision on these published reports. Therefore, they rely on the usefulness, accuracy and understandability of the *"intelligence"* provided.[5] *Bloomfield* cites a vivid example in which he compares financial reporting with the provision of raw data – it still depends on the investor himself to extract meaningful statistics out of the data and draw reasonable conclusions. This of course takes time and effort and is by no means a trivial task. Hence, the process is said to be costly. Still, the traditional Efficient Markets Hypothesis (EMH) leads to the conclusion that no matter how obscurely financial reports are presented or how costly their interpretation is, market prices fully reflect all available information. In contrast to the EMH, the Incomplete Revelation Hypothesis (IRH) states that investment decisions indeed depend on the extent of costs required to extract statistics from public data. It is argued that additional costs decrease trading interest. Low trading interest then leads to a lower revelation in market prices.[6] Moreover, and in line with the IRH, *Bloomfield* states that by various means managers could actively hamper investors to uncover information that should not be uncovered to keep stock prices high.[7] The IRH therefore implies that market reactions to negative business results can be reduced by providing information that is costly to analyze and interpret.[8]

---

[1] Baker/Kare (1992), p.1.
[2] Freeman (1984), p.46.
[3] Courtis (1995), p.4.
[4] Subramanian et al. (1993), p.49.
[5] Courtis (1995), p.4.
[6] Bloomfield (2002), pp.233.
[7] Bloomfield (2002), p.238.
[8] Bloomfield (2008), p.249.

One possible way of obscuring corporate information when results are negative, or of being forthcoming in disclosing information when results are good, is to adjust the reports' readability which can influence understandability as a consequence.[9] There is a broad set of readability formulas that allow defining a level of text difficulty based on linguistic factors like sentence length as well as word length and characteristics.[10] Careful application of these formulas allows providing an estimation of the probable success a target group will have in reading and understanding a certain text.[11] Various studies with different variables and samples have already shown that there are tendencies that weak financial performance induces poor readability of a report.[12] Still, it is doubtful whether reports are written to be difficult on purpose or it is just more demanding to explain why losses have occurred.[13] Moreover, numerous studies clearly disprove any significant relationship between performance and readability.[14] Additionally, the influence of a company's shareholder structure and the resulting dependence or independence of the management board on its financial report's readability is a topic that has not been examined adequately.

Most of the research conducted in the field of readability focuses on reports in English either as first or second language. Little attention has been paid to German reports. Besides of that it has always been the annual report being used as sample basis. Nonetheless, reports that are published throughout a business year, quarterly reports, should not be underestimated.

Therefore, the concrete aim of this study is to focus on the readability of letters to the shareholders of bilingual (German and English) quarterly reports of listed companies at Frankfurt Stock Exchange.

The underlying research question of this work shall be formulated as follows:

"What influences readability of letters to the shareholders of quarterly reports of publicly listed companies on the Frankfurt Stock Exchange?"

This study contributes to existing literature in various ways. On the one hand, it is among the very few works that consider the influence of performance on the readability of German reports and, in addition, sets the focus on quarterly reports. On the other hand, it takes into account the dependence or independence of managers of their shareholders measured by the company's shareholder structure, industry, share price volatility and the size of firms.

[9] Li (2008), p.221.
[10] Tekfi (1987), p.262.
[11] Courtis (1986), p.285.
[12] Adelberg (1979), Jones (1988), Baker and Kare (1992), Subramanian et al. (1993) and Li (2008)
[13] Bloomfield (2008), p.249.
[14] Courtis (1986), Rutherford (2003) and Smith et al. (2006)

Moreover, it is examined whether there is a tendency that reports in different languages tend to have the same relative level of difficulty. In general, the study also examines and questions research methods of prior studies in the field of report readability.

1.2 Structure

Chapter 2 gives the reader background on reporting habits and typical elements of content. The current legal and practical reporting situation at Frankfurt Stock Exchange is then discussed to become aware of what can actually be expected from published reports. Moreover, the Efficient Markets Hypothesis in contrast to the Incomplete Revelation Hypothesis is discussed to provide a theoretical basis why managers could offer (in)complete information in reports.

In **Chapter 3** the stakeholder theory is reviewed to gain understanding to whom company reports are addressed. Moreover, the status of shareholders is examined drawing on principal-agent theory and focusing on the question of how dependent or independent managers are from shareholders. The concept of obfuscation in reports is also discussed.

Chapter 4 explores the theoretical foundations of the empirical study and deeply reviews and compares existing literature and studies conducted in the field of readability. A special focus is set on prior research on readability of (annual) reports.

Then, in **Chapter 5**, the hypotheses are formulated and the research design for the empirical part is discussed. This also includes the presentation of the sample and the utilized variables. Moreover, the relevant statistical research methods are described.

Finally, in **Chapter** 6, various statistical analyses are conducted. The empirical results are then described, interpreted and compared with previous research. Besides, potential further fields of research are discussed. Moreover, the limitations of sample and methodology are discussed and evaluated.

In **Chapter 7**, a final conclusion is provided.

2. Reporting on Financial Markets

2.1 Introduction

Business participants, investors and all other types of stakeholders are familiar with the concept of annual reports. It is essentially *"a financial and narrative report"* of the firms' business activities during the previous year. The motivation to publish those reports is not solely based on a legal obligation since they also offer a suitable means for stakeholder communication.[15] Moreover, depending on local legislation, many listed companies are required to issue quarterly reports. These reports are often unaudited, less extensive and have very different levels of comprehensiveness. They are mainly designed to update existing, not prospective, shareholders.[16]

The following chapters elaborate on the functions, content and importance of both annual and quarterly reports. For reasons of simplicity and consistency with already existing literature, the term *reports* is used instead of *annual and quarterly reports* throughout this work with the exception of those sections where one type is meant specifically.

2.2 Purpose and Functions of Reports

Courtis provides a comprehensible definition of what (annual) reports are:[17]

"[...] a formal communication document comprising quantitative information, narratives, photographs and graphs. It seeks to inform shareholders, creditors and others [...]. It is essentially a response to mandatory disclosure requirements [...]. It is also a medium for voluntary disclosures perceived to produce net corporate benefits."

One can conclude from this quote that reports cannot be reduced to their sole existence due to legal obligations, but should be seen as a means of communication with stakeholders that allows assessing the risk-return ratio of an asset prior to an investment decision.[18]

Abstractly spoken, reports can be described as a *"costly process of information gathering and processing"*.[19] Broken down, reports merely serve the following functions:[20]

---

15 Stittle (2003), pp.3.
16 Downes/Goodman (2003), p.118.
17 Courtis (1995), p.4.
18 Courtis (1995), p.4.
19 Strieder (2003), p.34.
20 Strieder (2003), pp.35.

- **Information**
  - Self information
  - Information of shareholders, creditors and other stakeholders
  - Limited due to various measurement and assessment regulations
  - Limited due to obfuscation[21]
- **Protection of creditors**
  - Business risk of unsuccessful operation[22]
  - Risk of being ranked second after shareholders in terms of payments[23]
- **Justification**
  - Based on separation of ownership and control[24]
  - Documentation and evidence
- **Determination of income**
  - Based on balance sheet and income statement
  - Can be basis for tax calculation
  - Highly dependent on legal codes
- **Assessment of payments (e.g. dividends)**
  - Influenced by determined income and dividend policy
  - Regulated by capital maintenance rules

2.3 Typical Content of Reports

Jurisdiction usually requires companies to publish reports that contain at least a balance sheet and an income statement. Moreover, depending on specific law, a broad range of extensions and explanations is required.[25]

The factors influencing the concrete arrangement and content of reports are various. Typically, legal obligations, country, industry, firm size, habits and other factors are seen to play a crucial role. A rough separation of content into business reporting and financial reporting can be found in most reports.[26]

---

[21] Bloomfield (2008), p.249.
[22] Elliot/Elliot (2006), p.127.
[23] Elliot/Elliot (2006), p.127.
[24] Korn (1997), p.63.
[25] Strieder (2003), p.25.
[26] Stolowy/Lebas (2006), p.103.

Annual Report / Quarterly Report

First part: Business reporting

- Key financial information, highlights
- Letter from the president/CEO, letter to the shareholders, chairman's statement/address etc.
- Management report/review of operations (group, divisions, personnel, R&D etc.)
- Report of board of directors/management discussion and analysis/financial review (market evolution, group composition, earnings, production, personnel, capital expenditure, R&D, financing, shares, outlook, dividends etc.)

Second part: Financial reporting

- Consolidated financial statements (balance sheet, income statement, cash flow statement, statement of changes in equity)
- Notes to the consolidated financial statements
- Parent company financial statements (balance sheet, income statement, cash flow statement)
- Notes to the parent company financial statements
- Information on shares/shareholder information
- Report of the auditors
- Composition of the executive board/directors/corporate offices

2.3.1 Letter to the Shareholders

Since the letters to the shareholders form the sample basis for the present study, common characteristics of these letters are discussed in more detail in the following.

Typically, the letter to the shareholders[27] is said to be the *"most widely read and understood section of the report."*[28] Correspondingly, (potential) investors also base their investment decisions to a considerable extent on the content of the letters to the shareholders. The predictive strength of these letters concerning future results and possible failures has already been shown by studies. Analysts' forecasts and share prices are also affected by how letters to the shareholders are composed.[29] Critical voices see them as uncovered advertising measure.[30] *McConnell et al.* even describe them as *"documents with little, if any, substantive content"*.[31] Since publishing a letter to the shareholder is not mandatory, the concrete arrangement of content depends on the individual firm. Nevertheless, elements like introduction, revenues, finance and future outlook seem to be present frequently. Consequently, there exists a broad range of recommendations how to structure letters to the shareholders. One example is given below:[32]

- **Introduction**
- **Sales and earnings**
    - Sales, revenues and earnings results plus comparisons and explanations
- **Financial health**
    - Discussion of balance sheet, cash flow and capital structure
    - Explanation of changes
    - Dividends, stock splits, share repurchases etc.
- **Achievements**
    - Progress made on strategic goals
    - Link of operating performance and future results
- **Changes in management or board of directors**
    - Expression of appreciation

---

[27] often referred to as "letter from the president/CEO", "letter to the shareholder", "chairman's statement/address" etc.

[28] Balata/Breton (2005), p.5.

[29] Hooghiemstra (2010), pp.2.

[30] Smith/Taffler (2000), p.624.

[31] McConnel et al. (1986), p.66.

[32] The Heights (2013), slightly adapted

- **Outlook**
    - Future goals
    - Industry trends and market expectations
- **Closing**
    - Acknowledges for stakeholders
    - Date and signatures
    -

The structure recommended by *The Heights* is now applied to a randomly selected letter:

Dear Fellow Shareholders

2009 was an amazing year for Netflix. During the year, we added more than 2.8 million net new subscribers, continued to experience dramatic expansion and accelerating consumer adoption of our hybrid service combining streaming with DVDs by mail, and achieved strong gains in revenues and GAAP net income.

Outstanding growth
To put our subscriber growth into perspective: it took us four years, from 1999 to 2003, to reach our first million subscribers; in 2009, we added more than 1 million net new subscribers in the fourth quarter alone.

And we added subscribers at an increasing rate. Accelerating year-over-year subscriber growth is a clear sign consumers are embracing the Netflix value proposition of unlimited movies and TV episodes streamed over the Internet and on DVDs.

This subscriber growth translated into solid increases in revenues and net income. Revenue for 2009 increased 22 percent to $1.7 billion, and GAAP net income increased 40 percent to $115.9 million.

Focus on excellence
A key ingredient of our success is our persistent determination to deliver a truly excellent customer experience – an extensive content selection, a highly intuitive and useful Web site, outstanding customer service, and the most compelling value proposition.

That determination drove ongoing improvements to our movie recommendation algorithms, which means our subscribers more easily find movies they will love.

We also made improvements to DVD by mail. In 2009, we completed the nationwide rollout of Saturday shipping and continued to invest in automation for our distribution centers, which will improve service quality while reducing costs.

And we continued to enhance our streaming feature. In 2009, we added new, relevant content and new partnerships with consumer electronics manufacturers, ranging from Blu-ray players and Internet-connected TVs to game consoles, including Microsoft's Xbox 360 and Sony's PlayStation3. As a result, we expect to be embedded in nearly every Blu-ray player and Internet-connected TV sold in 2010.

Our subscribers have clearly engaged with streaming. In the fourth quarter of 2009, 48 percent of our subscribers instantly watched at least 15 minutes of a TV episode or movie, up from 28 percent a year earlier.

Looking ahead
We anticipate that the factors that contributed to our strong performance in 2009 will drive additional growth in 2010 and beyond. Those factors include the value proposition of our subscription model combining streaming with DVDs by mail, our persistent focus on delivering an outstanding customer experience and our growing ubiquity on Internet-connected devices that bring our streaming content to our subscribers' TVs, including Nintendo's Wii game console this spring.

Our long-term goals remain unchanged: To be a great Internet movie service by combining Internet delivery with DVD by mail, and to grow subscribers and earnings every year while continuing to invest in streaming. I am confident the innovation, skill and commitment of our employees will enable Netflix to extend our record of delivering an outstanding experience to our customers while creating value for our shareholders.

Sincerely,

Reed Hastings
Chief Executive Officer,
President and Co-founder

Figure 2: Typical content of a letter to the shareholders (Netflix, Inc. 2009, p.1. and The Height)

Letters to the shareholders are mostly not audited and not verified against the data that they refer to. Therefore, they can also be used as an instrument of impression management. Good results are usually described as the result of good internal strategy and investment behavior, whereas negative results are often attributed to external economic factors or other unforeseen events.[33] *Abrahamson and Amir* speak of the *"relative freedom in choosing the information reported in the president's letter and the lack of restrictions on the way the information is reported"*.[34]

2.4 Specifics of Reports at Frankfurt Stock Exchange Prime Market

2.4.1 The Frankfurt Stock Exchange

The very early history of Frankfurt Stock Exchange (FSE) dates back until 1150. The year 1585 is widely known as the natal hour FSE.[35]

Nowadays FSE is an important player in the world's financial markets. The traded securities are divided into three main levels of transparency, so-called *segments*:[36]

- **Prime Market** – A market regulated by the European Union that is mainly intended for companies that position themselves against an international investor base. Companies in this segment have to fulfill high requirements of transparency such as:
  - Quarterly reporting in German and English
  - IFRS/IAS or US-GAAP
  - Publication of a company calendar
  - At least one analysts' conference per year
  - Ad-hoc disclosures in German and English

  The Prime Market of FSE forms the basis of the sample that is used throughout the empirical part of this study.
- **General Standards** – A market regulated by the European Union that follows the minimum legal requirements. The requirements of transparency in this segment are lower and cover:
  - Ad-hoc disclosures
  - IFRS/IAS or US-GAAP
  - Publication of one interim report

[33] Hooghiemstra (2010) , p.2.
[34] Abrahamson/Amir (1996), p.1159.
[35] Website Frankfurter Wertpapierbörse (2013)
[36] Website Frankfurter Wertpapierbörse (2013)

- **Open Market** – The majority of traded securities in this segment are non-German. The market is not regulated by the European Union but by the stock exchange (regulated unofficial market).
- **Entry Standard** – A market that offers an alternative capital allocation for small and medium sized companies. It is not regulated by European Union transparency law but by the stock exchange. It forms part of the Open Market but has higher standards of transparency.

2.4.2 Annual Reports at Frankfurt Stock Exchange Prime Market

Section IV./2. of the directives of FSE regulates the publication of a *Jahresfinanzbericht* of companies listed on the Prime Market. § 50 (1) thereby refers to § 37v (2) WpHG which determines the minimum requirements of such a report:[37]

- An audited annual report according to national law of the company's country of residence
- Management report
- Declaration according to German Commercial Code (HGB) that the report has been prepared to the best of knowledge and judgment (so-called *Bilanzeid*)
- Proof on the entitlement of the auditor

The directive of FSE requires publishing both in German and in English. Companies with residence outside of Germany are allowed to provide annual reports solely in English. The reports have to be submitted four months after the respective period at the latest.[38] No regulatory obligation exists that claims the publication of a letter to the shareholders.
In general, all other regulatory laws remain unaffected. Exceptions granted by the Federal Financial Supervisory Authority (Bundesanstalt für Finanzdienstleistungsaufsicht) are valid, unless they contradict with basic ideas (*"tragende Gedanken"*) of the Prime Market.[39]

2.4.3 Quarterly Reports at Frankfurt Stock Exchange Prime Market

The directives of FSE regulate the publication of quarterly reports in § 51. Semi-annual reports (end of second quarter) underlie separate rules. Companies have to deliver quarterly reports that, according to §37w, comprise shortened financial statements and an interim management report.[40]

[37] Börsenordnung für die Frankfurter Wertpapierbörse (2013), pp.36. and WpHG (2013)
[38] Börsenordnung für die Frankfurter Wertpapierbörse (2013), p.37.
[39] Börsenordnung für die Frankfurter Wertpapierbörse (2013), p.37.
[40] Börsenordnung für die Frankfurter Wertpapierbörse (2013), p.37.

Quarterly reports must date at the end of the first and third quarters and have to be submitted within two months (three months if the residence lies outside of the European Economic Area). Regarding the language, the same rules apply as for annual reports.[41]

Quarterly reports can be audited on a voluntary basis. Different from annual and semi-annual reports, the auditors can be assigned by the management itself.[42]

2.5 Market Functioning

2.5.1 Introduction

Reports, as the primary means of communication between firms and shareholders, are crucial when it comes to investment decisions and the functioning of the capital market. The elementary role of this market is the allocation of ownership and resources in terms of capital. Investors base their investment decisions on the information that is provided. Nevertheless, it has to be scrutinized whether markets are *"efficient"* and *"fully reflect all available information"*.[43] Two hypotheses on market efficiency that are important for the course of this study are discussed below. Due to conflicting theoretical and empirical results, no conclusion on the accuracy of one model can be provided.[44]

2.5.2 Efficient Markets Hypothesis

The Efficient Markets Hypothesis represents a prime area of research in capital market theory.[45] The central statement of the hypothesis is that security markets are highly efficient in providing information about individual stocks and their sum.[46]

Efficiency in this respect is subject to the following three conditions:[47]

- No transaction costs are involved.
- All information available is obtainable without cost.
- An agreement exists that all information available is reflected by market prices.

As soon as new, market-relevant information arises, it is immediately reflected in the prices of securities. This happens by fast spreading of information without time delay. As a result, it is not possible to make advantage of buying or selling securities that are not priced correctly.[48]

---

[41] Börsenordnung für die Frankfurter Wertpapierbörse (2013), pp.37.
[42] Börsenordnung für die Frankfurter Wertpapierbörse (2013), p.38. and KPMG (2013)
[43] Fama (1970), p.383.
[44] Heiden (2006), p.54.
[45] Heun (2007), p.93.
[46] Malkiel (2003), p.59.
[47] Fama (1970), p.387.
[48] Malkiel (2003), p.59.

The hypothesis is historically based on the model of random walk which states that all price changes of securities are random in respect to their starting point. This also implies that future stock prices cannot be predicted since they are solely depending on information that is available in future. Past development also does not allow drawing conclusions about future expectations. Therefore, a completely inexperienced investor that buys stocks randomly would have the same rate of return as an expert.[49]

Based on the works of *Fama*, the following classification of information efficiency for capital markets can be set up:[50]

- Weak-form information efficient capital markets – current market prices reflect all information on *past* price developments (poor empirical validation)
- Semi-strong-form information efficient capital markets – current market prices reflect all *current publicly available* information (empirical validation)
- Strong-form information efficient capital markets – current market prices reflect all *publicly available and private* information (falsified)

Despite its popularity gained in the 1970s, the Efficient Markets Hypothesis nowadays underlies criticism among scholars.[51] Having reviewed a broad range of previous studies, *Heun* concludes that the existence of strong-form information efficient capital markets has to be denied. For semi-strong and weak form information efficient markets the empirical validations point out the practical limitations of the theory. The semi-strong form is empirically best proven. Moreover, the model of random walk is empirically not validated.[52]

Bloomfield summarizes *"The EMH* [Efficient Markets Hypothesis] *has been highly influential among academics, but practitioners and regulators appear unconvinced."*[53]

2.5.3 Incomplete Revelation Hypothesis

The Incomplete Revelation Hypothesis developed by *Bloomfield* is theoretically based on the *noisy expectations* model by *Grossman and Stiglitz*.[54] Rational agents can freely decide to collect information on the value of an asset. If they decide to do so and then trade the asset, they are confronted with *noise* traders that trade randomly. These noise traders are the reason why market prices do not reveal information completely. For example, if a noise trader sells extensively, the resulting drop in market prices does not come from negative company news that is obtained by informed traders, but from the random behavior of noise traders.

---

[49] Malkiel (2003), pp.59.
[50] Fama (1970), p.414., Shleifer (2000), p.6. and Scheufele/Haas (2008), p.27.
[51] Shleifer (2000), pp.9.
[52] Heun (2007), p.95.
[53] Bloomfield (2002), p.233.
[54] Bloomfield (2002), p.234. and Heiden (2006), p.56.

Consequently, the market heads to an equilibrium between traders that collect information (at cost) and traders that decide not to do so. Informed trading only results in limited gains since the amount of gain decreases, the more informed traders are active. Therefore, it depends on a cost-benefit ratio whether to search for and analyze information or not. *Bloomfield*, instead of referring to the number of information-collecting traders, speaks of *trading interest*. It is defined as the willingness to trade, if the market price deviates from the value that is identified based on available information and its statistics.[55]

The practical link of this equilibrium is described by *Bloomfield* by referring to the difference between data and statistics:[56]

"Data are ink spots on sheets of paper [...] Statistics are the useful facts extracted from that data, such as earnings figures and financial ratios. While public data are often free, it takes time and effort to extract statistics [...]."

The Incomplete Revelation Hypothesis subsequently states that the more costly it is to extract statistics about securities on capital markets, the less those statistics induce price changes. It is argued that information extraction costs decrease trading interest. Low trading interest then leads to a lower revelation in market prices. In contrast, the Efficient Markets Hypothesis does not consider the reaction of prices based on the extraction costs of statistics due to its disregard of transaction costs.[57] Concerning share price volatility, the Incomplete Revelation Hypothesis does not yet provide an explanatory problem-solving approach.

Seen globally, *Bloomfield's* position reflects an intermediary position between supporters and critics of the Efficient Markets Hypothesis. On the one hand, inefficiencies are tolerated; on the other hand, market players act rationally.[58] Most importantly, the model considers the effect of demand and supply of financial information on prices.[59]

Practical implications of the Incomplete Revelation Hypothesis on reporting mentioned by *Bloomfield* target managers' desire to keep stock prices at a high level or increase them. Therefore, they partially make decisions that reduce the ease of uncovering and analyzing information which mitigate the influence on share prices. Typical decisions would be:[60]

- Promotion of accounting methods that improve popular statistics like earnings-per-share and debt-equity ratio and ensconce expenses and liabilities in footnotes
- Presentation of extraordinary gains as operating gains and ongoing expenses as extraordinary expenses

---

[55] Bloomfield (2002), pp.234.
[56] Bloomfield (2002), p234.
[57] Bloomfield (2002), pp.235.
[58] Heiden (2006), p.56.
[59] Heiden (2006), p.58.
[60] Bloomfield (2002), p.238.

- Announcement of pro forma performance figures that are compared to strategically chosen previous figures
- Generation of hidden reserves to keep up positive results in tensed times

Essential for this study is the obfuscation of information by adjusting the readability of corporate disclosures. The obfuscation hypothesis is discussed in chapter 3.5.2.

3. Stakeholder Theory

3.1 Historical Origins

The modern interpretation of the term *stakeholder* dates back until 1963 when it was used internally at the Stanford Research Institute (SRI) and referred to the fact that shareholders are not the only interest group of companies.[61] Stakeholders were seen as *"those groups without whose support the organization would cease to exist"* by the SRI.[62]

Notwithstanding the above, the topic itself was already considered earlier. Actually, already *Adam Smith* (1759 and 1776) provides a framework of considering the necessity of a coalition between economic and ethical interests. According to *Smith*, this symbiosis results in the best functioning of society.[63] Interestingly, *Smith* is sometimes misunderstood as a pure proponent of shareholder value based on his concept of the invisible hand (*The Wealth of Nations*). Yet this is just one side of the coin of *Smith's* work. Especially in the light of his work *Theory of Moral Sentiments*, which sets a focus on morality, justice and beneficence, this strict point of view has to be denied.[64]

Wentges names *Berle and Means* (1932), *Dodd* (1932), *Barnard* (1938) and *March and Simon* (1958) as scholars of the 20th century that provide essential conceptual input for later work. The key message in their works is the need for balancing the interests of various groups.[65]

Nevertheless, it is *Freeman* in the 1980s who initiates contemporary discussion and research amongst academics and the link to strategic management.[66]

3.2 Stakeholder Definition

Besides the early definition from 1963 mentioned above, the term *stakeholder* is often depicted in various other ways. The list of different definitions is nearly endless and leads to unnecessary confusion.[67]

Freeman and Reed (1983) propose to separately define stakeholders in a wider and narrower sense:[68]

61 Parmar/Freeman et al. (2010), p.405.
62 Freeman/Reed (1983), p.89.
63 Andriof et al. (2002), p.10.
64 Brown/Forster (2013), pp.301.
65 Wentges (2002), pp.88.
66 Parmar/Freeman et al. (2010), pp.405.
67 Miles (2012), p.285.

"Any identifiable group or individual who can affect the achievement of an organization's objectives or who is affected by the achievements of an organization's objective." (definition in the wide sense)

"Any identifiable group or individual on which the organization is dependent for its continued survival." (definition in the narrow sense)

Freeman (1984) states a very similar, often cited, definition shortly thereafter:[69]

"A stakeholder in an organization is (by definition) any group or individual who can affect or is affected by the achievement of the organization's objectives."

Clarkson (1995) draws a separating line between primary and secondary stakeholders and defines as follows:[70]

"A primary stakeholder group is one without whose continuing participation the corporation cannot survive as a going concern. Primary stakeholder groups typically are comprised of shareholders and investors, employees, customers, and suppliers [...]"

"Secondary stakeholder groups are defined as those who influence or affect, or are influenced or affected by, the corporation, but they are not engaged in transactions with the corporation and are not essential for its survival."

Post et al. (2002) state:[71]

"The stakeholders in a corporation are the individuals and constituencies that contribute, either voluntarily or involuntarily, to its wealth-creating capacity and activities, and that are therefore its potential beneficiaries and/or risk bearers."

Along with the definitions of stakeholders mentioned above, one can set up a list of potential resources that can be at stake for the stakeholders:[72]

- Capital resources – equity, liabilities, real estates, workforce, natural resources
- Trust – social acceptance and good working environment
- Information and know-how

---

68 Freeman/Reed (1983), p.91.
69 Freeman (1984), p.46.
70 Clarkson (1995), pp.106.
71 Post et al. (2002), p.19.
72 Figge/Schaltegger (2000), p.11.

3.3 Stakeholder Groups

Despite the existence of both narrow and broad definitions and classifications of stakeholders, some groups tend to be involved by most of the definitions. Among them shareholders naturally occupy a special and central position.

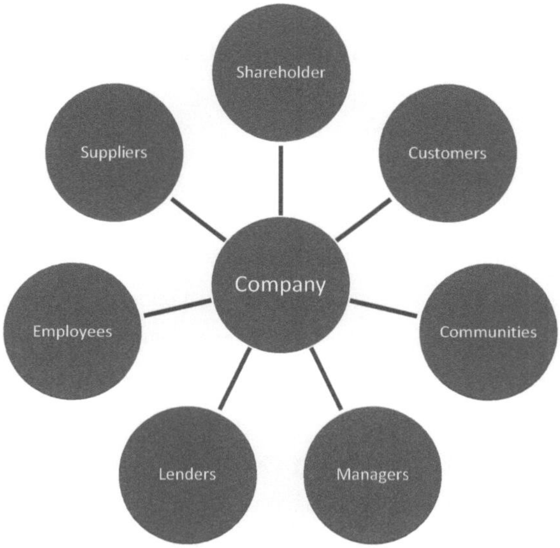

Figure 3: Typical stakeholders of a company (Parmar/Freeman et al. 2010, p.406.)

3.4 Stakeholder Concept

The stakeholder concept is a concept of analysis of strategic management. It is based on the insight that the majority of companies are no longer solely in the possession of a few individuals. Instead, they have to be interpreted as quasi-public institutions and form a place of exchange of conflicting and complementary interests of various internal and external stakeholders.[73] These institutions form a coalition between stakeholders that have financial investments and those who do not. Stakeholders with no financial investment also play a crucial role in the link between corporate strategy and finance.[74] By the pragmatic approach of focusing (solely) on the needs of their stakeholders, companies can be most effective in accomplishing their strategic objectives.[75]

[73] Figge/Schaltegger (2000), p.11.
[74] Cornell/Shapiro (1987), p.5.
[75] Freeman (1999), p.234.

The key questions that are addressed by the stakeholder concept in connection with strategic management are:[76]

- How can value be created in rapidly changing societies?
- What is the relation between capitalism and ethics?
- What is managers' mindset in the tradeoff and relation between profit and ethics?

3.5 Relationship Between Shareholders and Managers

3.5.1 Agency Theory

In the construct of a company, shareholders, managers and especially their cooperation occupy a central role in value creation. From a theoretical perspective the relationship between these two stakeholders can be well described with the agency theory[77]. This theory ties in with the stakeholder theory by considering the situation when cooperating parties have different goals and delegation is involved.[78] Consequently, the relationship between shareholders and managers represents a situation of *"separation of ownership and control"* that is based on contractual arrangements.[79] The shareholder as the principal decides to delegate managerial tasks to his agent, namely the manager.[80] Nevertheless, agency theory must not be reduced to shareholders and managers. It has to be interpreted in a broad context and encompasses relationships that are based on delegation and representation:[81]

"Essentially all contractual arrangements, as between employer and employee or the state and the governed, for example, contain important elements of agency."

The aim of agency theory is to resolve two main problems that can arise due to the existence of information asymmetry and conflictual, opportunistic behaviour. These can be conflicting interests between principal and agent as well as the difficulty and expense to screen the actions of the agent on the one hand. On the other hand, the two parties' risk preferences need not to be equal which in turn leads to divergent preference actions.[82] Due to the fact that both attempt to maximize their utility, it is reasonable to assume that the agent does not always act in the very best interest of his principal. By using incentive measures and monitoring, these divergences can be partly reduced. Nevertheless, this induces costs and does not align all actions of the agent.[83] The total costs of agency comprise of:[84]

---

[76] Parmar/Freeman et al. (2010), pp.405.
[77] often referred to as "principal-agent problem"
[78] Jensen/Meckling (1976), p.308.
[79] Jensen/Meckling (1976), p.309.
[80] Jensen/Mecking (1976), p.310.
[81] Ross (1973), p.134.
[82] Eisenhardt (1989), pp.58.
[83] Jensen/Meckling (1976), p.308.

- Monitoring expenditures – controlling the agent's behavior through rules, policies and restrictions
- Bonding expenditures – contractual costs of the agent
- Residual loss – costs that arise from the difference between the agent's decision and the decision that would maximize the principal's welfare (opportunity costs)

3.5.2 Obfuscation Hypothesis

Based on the concept of information asymmetry between managers and investors, the obfuscation hypothesis describes a situation where the former underscore their successes and obfuscate their failures. The hypothesis finds a special application in readability research and questions whether disclosures with good results are written more readably than disclosures with negative results.[85] Obfuscation *"obscures the intended message, or confuses, distracts or perplexes readers, leaving them bewildered or muddled."*[86] Consequently, reports with poor readability decrease investors' motivation to dig deeper and investigate more precisely.[87] Intentional obfuscation typically arises through the usage of:[88]

- Esoteric or obscurantist vocabulary
- Jargon
- Irrelevant information
- Complex and long sentences
- High variability in reading ease
- Overlapping and spurious argumentation

3.5.3 Shareholder Influence and Independence

The degree of effectiveness of monitoring (expenditures) in agency theory depends on how much influence shareholders can exert on the management or how independent managers are from their principals. While this conclusion tends to be rather trivial, measuring or qualifying the degree of independence is certainly not.

A first practical attempt to solve this issue is made by the *Bureau van Dijk* with its BvDEP Independence Indicator. It aims *"to characterise the degree of independence of a company with regard to its shareholders."*[89]

---

[84] Jensen/Meckling (1976), p.308.
[85] Courtis (1998), pp.461.
[86] Courtis (2004), p.292.
[87] Courtis (1998), pp.461.
[88] Courtis (2004), p.292.
[89] Bureau van Dijk (2008), p.15.

The indicator is solely based on information about ownership structure and therefore does not question how shareholders are organized or which alliances exist between them. Small-scaled investors[90], which are typically stated aggregately, are not considered in the calculation since they are assumed to have no effective controlling power over a company.[91]
To fully understand the definitions of the main groups of independence, it is necessary to get acquainted with the different types of ownership that are used by the indicator:[92]

- Direct ownership – A owns a certain percentage of B
- Indirect ownership – A owns B through another entity
- Total ownership – A owns of B through direct and indirect ownership
- Calculated total ownership (control) – Concept which follows the IFRS concept of control *"and calculates a total percentage by making the sum of the direct percentages of all minority direct shareholders controlled by the same controlling company."*

This independence indicator knows five main levels of independence ranging from "A" to "D" with "U" reserved for unknown levels of independence. "A" refers to situations where managers are relatively independent from shareholders and can expect little influence, whereas "D" represents a situation of low independence from shareholders.[93]

[90] often referred to as "public investors", "private investors", "other individuals" or "unnamed shareholders"
[91] Bureau van Dijk (2008), p.15.
[92] Bureau van Dijk (2008), p.6.
[93] Bureau van Dijk (2008), p.15.

Independence Level	Definition
A	No shareholder has more than 25% direct or total ownership
B	No shareholders has more than 50% direct, total or calculated total ownership, at least one shareholder has more than 25% direct, total or calculated total ownership
C	Shareholder with more than 50% total or calculated total ownership
D	Shareholder with more than 50% direct ownership
U	None of the above, unknown

Table 1: BvDEP Independence Indicator classification (Bureau van Dijk 2008, pp.15.)

4. Readability Research

4.1 Concept of Readability

The concept of readability has been described by a number of authors. *Dale and Chall* characterize readability as:

"[...] the sum total (including interactions) of all those elements within a given piece of printed material that affects the success, which a group of readers have with it. The success is the extent to which they understand it, read it at optimum speed, and find it interesting."[94]

In simple terms, readability describes the ease with which a text can be read and understood.[95] The underlying premise that readability also reflects understandability has substantiated a broad range of studies. Some researches even treat readability and understandability as synonyms.[96] Others argue in favor of a clear linguistic separation.[97] *Smith and Taffler* mark that they are *"[...] different concepts [...] and that synonymous treatment [...] is not justified."*[98] It is generally said that readability focuses on the problem of matching text and reader and therefore explains the effectiveness of written communication.[99]

According to *Dale and Chall,* the variables that influence the readability of a passage are an accumulation of comprehension, interest and fluency. Comprehension describes the reader's capability to understand, while interest refers to the level of motivation to continue reading a certain text. Fluency determines the capacity to read at the most favorable speed.[100] Reader's comprehension in this respect is defined trough elements like content, style, format and organization.[101]

An alternative, more qualitative definition of readability is provided by *Lesikar.* If one can understand the intended message of a text on the first reading attempt, the text is said to be readable. Besides of that, the effort of the reader is minimal and the intended message reaches the reader free of error.[102]

Still, neither the definitions by *Dale and Chall* nor by *Lesikar* provide clear characteristics that allow differentiating between a readable and an unreadable text.

A comprehensive overview of what potentially influences reading difficulty is given by *Oakland and Lane:*

---

[94] Dale/Chall (1949), p.23.
[95] Oakland/Lane (2004), p.244.
[96] Jones (1988), pp.297.
[97] Smith/Taffler (1992), pp.84.
[98] Smith/Taffler (1992), p.91.
[99] Lewis et al. (1986), pp.199.
[100] Dale/Chall (1948), pp.13.
[101] Courtis (1986), p.285.
[102] Mohamad/Rahman (2006), p.35.

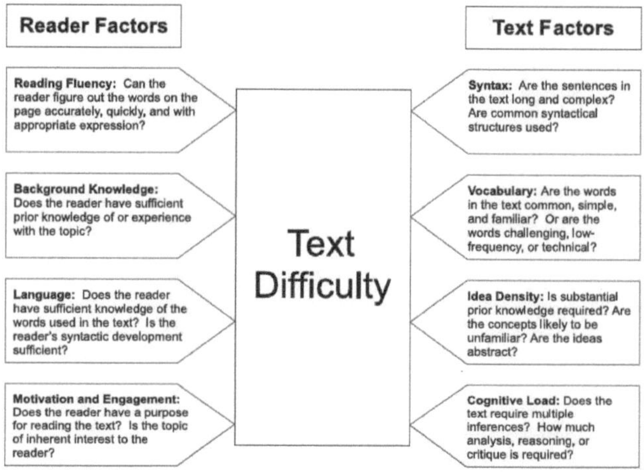

Figure 4: Factors that influence reading difficulty (Oakland/Lane 2004, p.248.)

4.2 Measures of Readability

4.2.1 Introduction

"[...] readability formulas do not define readability. They measure factors which can correlate with difficulty [...]."[103]

Transforming a text into a single indicator that describes its readability is a challenging task which requires simplification and concentration on a few characteristics. It depends on the underlying formula's ability to consider elements of writing that are related to comprehension (content, style, format and organization) how successful and useful a given result is. In this respect it is only the style element that can be measured in a practical way.[104] One should always keep in mind *Robert Gunning's* quote:[105]

"No formula will guarantee that you write well. Nonsense written simply is still nonsense."

Typically, formulas that consider two text-related variables of style are used: The semantic variable word length, for example, is regarded as an indicator of the speed of recognition during the reading process. Sentence length, a syntactic variable, is linked to the memory span of the reader. Although it is sentence complexity that induces reading difficulty, sentence

[103] Dreyer (1984), p.335.
[104] Courtis (1986), p.285.
[105] Gunning (1969), p.12.

length may be used as a proxy. However, for both word and sentence length it is important to consider that they do not cause difficulty or readability, but solely represent good indices.[106] Most of the readability measures attempt to define the minimum reading age to understand a certain text or the difficulty that is typical for a certain level of education. Some are originally also intended to be used for children.[107] Today the list of readability formulas is nearly endless. Already by 1982, *Kare* counted more than 200 of them.[108] An overview of the most influential measures that can be applied for adults is provided below.

4.2.2 Historical Overview of Readability Research

Around 2,900 years ago the Talmudists counted both the number of word appearance as well as individual ideas in their texts. Their intention was to compare the appearance of these factors in an unusual and usual sense.[109]

By the end of the 19th century the Russian scientist *Nikolai Aleksandrovich Rubakin* pursued a word frequency study based on thousands of texts written by soldiers, artisans and agriculturists. He finally drew up a list of 1,500 words that seemed easy enough to be understood by the majority of the population. *Rubakin* concluded that the main reasons why people cannot read texts properly are the usage of uncommon vocabulary and long sentences.[110]

Sherman's publication about sentence study of English literature from 1893 is very influential for later readability formulas. He notices the effect of progressive shortening of sentences throughout the history of literature. Early writers like *Geoffrey Chaucer* (14th century) write with an average sentence length of 50 words, whereas *William Ellery Channing* (19th century) has an average sentence length of around 24 words. His equation of sentence length and readability, which was also confirmed by later studies, is of key importance for the usage of sentence length in most readability formulas that emerged later on. Moreover, *Sherman* discovers that some writers have a quite constant length of sentences which supports the trend to use samples instead of the entire work. Most importantly *Sherman* concludes that it is essential to recognize the reader and his abilities during the process of writing. Many studies that are later conducted agree with this notion.[111]

4.2.3 Gray and Leary's Readability Study (1935)

---

[106] Courtis (1986), pp.285.
[107] Tekfi (1987), p.267.
[108] DuBay (2004), p.42. Crossley et al. (2007) only count more than 50
[109] Tekfi (1987), p.263.
[110] Tekfi (1987), p.263.
[111] Tekfi (1987), p.264.

Gray and Leary use experts' opinion to gain insights which factors influence the readability of books. They conduct a survey with cooperation of librarians, teachers and publishers and come up with 228 potential characteristics of reading ease that can be grouped into content, style, format and organization. Since all basic elements cannot be measured except of style, they focus on 64 variables of style that can be counted reliably.[112] To specify if the factors are connected to reading ease, the authors use a reading comprehension test that is pursued with around 1,000 participants. 17 out of this 64 variables show a significant correlation (>0.35) between variable change and perceived change in textual difficulty.[113]

Number	**Factor**	**Correlation Coefficient**
1	*Average sentence length*	-0.52
2	Percentage of easy words	+0.52
3	Number of words unknown to 6th grade students	-0.51
4	Number of easy words	+0.51
5	*Number of different hard words*	-0.50
6	Minimum syllabic sentence length	-0.49
7	Number of explicit sentences	+0.48
8	*Number of 1st, 2nd and 3rd pronouns*	+0.48
9	Maximum syllabic sentence length	-0.47
10	Average syllabic sentence length	-0.47
11	Percentage of monosyllables	+0.43
12	Number of sentences per paragraph	+0.43
13	Percentage of different words unknown to 6th grade pupils	-0.40
14	Number of simple sentences	+0.39
15	*Percentage of different words*	-0.38
16	Percentage of polysyllables	-0.38

[112] DuBay (2004), pp.40.
[113] Tekfi (1987), p.267.

17	*Number of prepositional phrases*	-0.35

Table 2: List of style factors affecting readability by Gray and Leary (Lekfi 1987, p.267.)

Aware of the fact that correlation coefficients between 0.35 and 0.52 are not extraordinarily high, *Gray and Leary* search for elements that are highly predictive but not related to each other to increase explanatory power. The finally come up with a formula that uses five of the above mentioned variables: numbers 1, 5, 8, 15 and 17. Adding another variable would only lead to a minimally increased accuracy but to more complexity and more difficult application.[114]

It is not the formula built by *Gray and Leare* itself that highly influences later research, but their stimulation for other academics to find better formulas based on their data.[115]

4.2.4 Dale-Chall Formula (1948)

The formula developed by *Dale and Chall* estimates readability of English texts in terms of grades of school based on a set of 3,000 words that they consider to be best known by 8-year-old children in the United States. This list is based on 30 rules that decide whether a word is familiar for a child or not.[116] It is primarily seen as a list of words that have high correlation with reading difficulty, but does not represent a set of the most important words for children or adults.[117] Moreover, the formula considers sentence length as the second factor of readability.[118]

[114] DuBay (2004), p.42.
[115] DuBay (2004), p.42.
[116] Lewis et al. (1986), p.200.
[117] DuBay (2004), p.84.
[118] Lewis et al. (1986), p.200.

Dale List of 3,000 Words

a	ah	an	armful	awhile	barrel
able	ahead	and	army	ax	base
aboard	aid	angel	arose	baa	baseball
about	aim	anger	around	babe	basement
above	air	angry	arrange	baby (ies).	basket
absent	airfield	animal	arrive (d)	back	bat
accept	airport	another	arrow	background	batch
accident	airplane	answer	art	backward (s)	bath
account	airship	ant	artist	bacon	bathe
ache (ing)	airy	any	as	bad (ly)	bathing
acorn	alarm	anybody	ash (es)	badge	bathroom
acre	alike	anyhow	aside	bag	bathtub
across	alive	anyone	ask	bake (r)	battle
act	all	anything	asleep	baking	battleship
add	alley	anyway	at	bakery	bay
address	alligator	anywhere	ate	ball	be (ing)
admire	allow	apart	attack	balloon '	beach
adventure	almost	apartment	attend	banana	bead
afar	alone	ape	attention	band	beam
afraid	along	apiece	August	bandage	bean
after	aloud	appear	aunt	bang	bear
afternoon	already	apple	author	banjo	beard
afterward (s)	also	April	auto	bank (er)	beast
again	always	apron	automobile	bar	beaming
against	am	are	autumn	barber	beautiful
age	America	aren't	avenue	bare (ly)	beautify
aged	American	arise	awake (n)	barefoot	beauty
ago	among	arithmetic	away	bark	became
agree	amount	arm	awful (ly)	barn	because

Figure 5: Exemplary excerpt of words contained in Dale's list (DuBay 2004, p.85)

The formula itself is defined as follows:[119]

Raw score = (0.1579 * percentage of unfamiliar words) + (0.0496 * average number of words per sentence)

The resulting raw score can be transferred to the corrected US grade levels by the help of the following table:

Formula Raw Score	Corrected US Grade-levels
4.9 and below	4th grade and below
5.0 to 5.9	5-6th grade
6.0 to 6.9	7-8th grade
7.0 to 7.9	9-10th grade
8.0 to 8.9	11-12th grade
9.0 to 9.9	13-15th grade (college)
10.0 and above	16-(college graduate)

Table 3: Dale-Chall formula correction table (DuBay 2004, p.81.)

[119] Lewis et al. (1986), p.200.

The following sample text with unfamiliar words italicized would result in a raw score of 6.35 and a corrected US grade level of 7-8:[120]

> *Diphtheria* used to kill many babies. Today no child need die [sic] of *diphtheria*. It is one of the *diseases* for which we have very good *treatment* and almost sure prevention. But your baby will not be safe from this *disease* unless he has been protected by *immunization.*
>
> The way to protect your baby is simple. *Physicians usually* give *injections* of three *doses* of *toxoid*, three to four weeks apart, generally beginning when a baby is about six months old. Your doctor will tell you that your baby should have this *protection* before his first birthday.
>
> Six months after the last *injection* of *toxoid*, the *physician* may test your baby to see if another *dose* of *toxoid* is *necessary*. Before the child enters school an extra shot of *toxoid* is often given.

For sample collection *Dale and Chall* recommend extracting 100-word passages from every tenth page from books and four 100-word samples every 2,000 words from articles. A sample should never begin or end within a sentence. Unfamiliar words that appear more than once should be counted according to their appearance. Other more detailed rules concerning treatment of verbs, adjectives, adverbs, irregular plural of familiar singular words, names and persons, abbreviations, suffixes and numbers are also provided but are not discussed in detail here.[121]

The Dale-Chall formula was already validated in the early 1950s.[122]

4.2.5 Gunning-Fog Index (1952)

The Fog index, developed by *Robert Gunning*, describes the readability of a document as a function of the amount of words per sentence and the amount of syllables per word. A well-formed and logical text has to be assumed.[123]

The Fog index formula is defined as follows:

$$\text{Fog index} = (\text{average words per sentence} + \text{percentage of complex words}) * 0.4$$

---

[120] DuBay (2004), p.82.
[121] DuBay (2004), pp.75.
[122] Bickley et al. (1970), p.233.
[123] Lehavy (2011), pp.1093.

According to *Gunning's* formula, a complex word contains at least three syllables. The resulting index estimates the number of formal years of education of an average intelligent reader who is able to read and understand the text.

The resulting Fog index can be interpreted and compared with the help of the following table:

Fog Index	Category
19.5	Technical books
17.0	Scientific literature
13.7	Newspapers
12.6	Instruction manuals
9.7	General circulation magazines
8.6	Youth magazines

Table 4: Interpretation of the Fog index (Courtis 1995, p.7.)

The example text from chapter 4.2.4 results in a Fog index of 9.8 – a level slightly above an average general circulation magazine.[124]

Gunning's Fog index has been validated with a correlation coefficient of 0.50 with *McCall-Crabbs'* Standard Lessons in Reading.[125]

4.2.6 Flesch Index (1948)

Rudolf Flesch, a Viennese, starts working in the field of readability after his immigration to the US in 1938. He publishes a relatively simple formula in his dissertation in 1943. *Flesch* presents an updated formula for measuring reading ease in his work *"A New Readability Yardstick"* in 1948 and starts a revolution in journalism and business communication. His updated formula proposes 100-word samples and only consists of two variables: number of syllables and sentence length.[126] The Flesch index primarily aims to measure readability of adult reading material.[127]

The Flesch index is calculated as follows:[128]

Flesch index = 206.835 – (84.6 * average number of syllables per word) – (1.015 * average number of words per sentence)

[124] Readability-score.com (2013)
[125] Courtis (1986), p.286.
[126] DuBay (2004), p.96.
[127] Lewis et al. (1986), p.200.
[128] DuBay (2004), p.97.

Flesch points out that for interpretation of the formula one has to realize that word length and sentence length are proxies for word complexity. Subsequently, word and sentence complexity are a measure for abstraction.[129]

Typical results range from 0 to 100 whereas a low result indicates a high reading difficulty. Results below or above the mentioned range may occur.[130]

The author also develops a table that helps interpreting obtained results:

Reading Ease Score	Style Description	Typical Magazine	Estimated Reading Grade	Estimated % of U.S. Adults (1949)
0 to 30	Very difficult	Scientific	College graduate	4.5
30 to 50	Difficult	Academic	13th to 16th grade	33
50 to 60	Fairly difficult	Quality	10th to 12th grade	54
60 to 70	Standard	Digests	8th and 9th grade	83
70 to 80	Fairly easy	Slick-fiction	7th grade	88
80 to 90	Easy	Pulp-fiction	6th grade	91
90 to 100	Very easy	Comics	6th grade	93

Table 5: Flesch' reading ease scale (DuBay 2004, p.97. and Flesch 1948, p.230.)

The example text from chapter 4.2.4 results in a Flesch index of 63.1 which is a standard difficulty that should be understood by most people.[131]

An often mentioned empirical validation of the Flesch index is its correlation coefficient of 0.70 with the Standard Test Lessons in Reading by *McCall-Crabbs.*[132]

4.3 Limitations of Readability Measures

4.3.1 Introduction

Readability formulas developed in the last centuries have had a considerable impact on both public and private life. Educational reading material, insurance policies, contracts, remedial reading texts and basal series may be checked with the help of readability formulas. Still it

[129] Flesch (1948), p.225.
[130] DuBay (2004), p.97.
[131] Readability-score.com (2013)
[132] Courtis (1986), p.286.

has to be questioned if the formulas *"fulfill their promise"*.[133] In general, the formulas are seen to predict the level of reading ease in a questionable way and fail to assess the cause of difficulty.[134]

4.3.2 Bruce's Categorization

Bruce et al. categorize the key problems with readability measures as follows:

- **Neglected factors:**
  This limitation refers to the discrepancy between variables that are measured and variables that are known to influence the readability of a text. Factors such as degree of discourse cohesions, number of inferences required, amount of items to remember, idea complexity and rhetorical structure are not considered in a proper way.[135] Moreover, they criticize the harsh separation of reading material and reader which does not allow respecting dialect, reader's knowledge background, motivation and interests. Importantly, *Bruce et al.* mention the factor reading time which is probably very essential in reading and understanding of texts.[136]
- **Lack of statistical basis:**
  Besides of their lack of theoretical foundation, readability formulas also have severe flaws in their practical derivation. Most formulas are based on earlier, already existing formulas that are derived from statistical tests like *McCall-Crabbs'* Standard Test Lessons in Reading or *Gray and Leary's* readability studies. Especially the first was never meant to be a measure of text comprehensibility and an indicator of reading ability depending on demographic characteristics. *Bruce et al.* indicate that various studies have proven the inefficiency of reading formulas but "positive" results tend to be published more often in journals. It is also emphasized that readability formulas based on (old) statistics need to be adopted constantly to account for changing data.[137] *Redish* stresses that generalizing from testing situations that are decades old and of indirect relevance to the reader and type of reading material is incorrect since *"The formulas are out of date."*[138]

---

[133] Bruce et al. (1981), p.50.
[134] Redish (2000), p.132.
[135] cf. chapter 4.2.3
[136] Bruce et al. (1981), pp.50.
[137] Bruce et al. (1981), pp.50.
[138] Redish (2000), p.133.

- **Inappropriate use:**

  Firstly, due to the enormous simplification methods of the formulas that do not consider content, texts of simplicity in style but complexity in content could be seen as suitable for education and be introduced in lessons. If this happens, the application of the formula fails.[139]

  Secondly, readability formulas and their underlying variables are often misinterpreted as guidelines to increase reading ease. The conclusion of a writer could for example be: The shorter the sentence, the easier the text may be read. This conclusion totally neglects that sentence length is only an indicator for reading difficulty. *Bruce et al.* therefore state:[140]

  > *"Although they* [the readability formulas] *may, in certain cases, assign reasonable numerical values to texts, they by no means justify modifications of an existing text."*

  Klare compares the act of "improving" readability with the help of formulas with increasing a room's temperature by lighting a match beneath the thermometer. The index changes, reality does not.[141] In fact both *Gunning* and *Flesch* insist that their formulas should not be misused for revision purpose.[142]

4.3.3 Other Critics

Crossley et al. criticize the absence of underlying theory and the sole focus on correlation studies based on tests with students in setting up the majority of readability formulas. This fact makes them weak in principle and aggravates their application for technical texts.[143]

A point that is not explicitly mentioned by *Bruce et al.* is how the text is graphically organized. Elements like graphs, imagery, font size and font type are typically not considered.[144]

Per definition readability formulas rely on variables that can be counted. *Redish* lists other key questions concerning readability that have not yet been integrated to formulas:

---

[139] Bruce et al. (1981), pp.50.
[140] Bruce et al. (1981), p.51.
[141] Redish (2000), p.136.
[142] Redish (2000), p.136.
[143] Crossley et al. (2007), p.197.
[144] Redish (2000), p.134.

Is the content right for the audience?
Is the document organized so that users can find what they need?
Are there any headings? Are the headings meaningful and useful to the audience?
Is there a table of contents? Is it useful?
Is there an index? Does it have users' words in it?
Does the page layout help users find what they need?
Are there visuals (tables, charts, screenshots, and lists) to help users?
Is the text divided into short sections and paragraphs (chunks) so that users are invited to use them?
Are the sentences grammatical?
Are the words ones that these users know?

Table 6: Key questions unanswered by readability formulas (Redish 2000, pp.134.)

She concludes the list with the statement:[145]

"Given this long list, it is difficult to see why anyone would want to limit the definition of a 'readable' document to 'short sentences' and 'simple words' the features counted by readability formulas."

Smith and Taffler question if readability formulas are designed to measure readability and/or understandability and argue that this actually makes a difference. In contrast to *Adelberg and Razek* they would not treat them as synonyms.[146] This point of view questions the sense of readability formulas and their application in many situations.

Besides all their limitations and critics, traditional readability formulas still enjoy great popularity and are widely used in today's research. *Redish and Selzer* already warned back in 1985:[147]

"Readability formulas are seductive. They are easy to learn, easy to use, and inexpensive. They require no involvement from other people [...]. They give an impartial and objective measure. Computerization makes the formulas even easier to use. [...] We are concerned that the temptation to rely on computer programs [...] can become overwhelming."

---

[145] Redish (2000), p.135.
[146] Smith/Taffler (1992), pp.84.
[147] Redish/Selzer (1985), p.46.

4.3.4 Alternatives

4.3.4.1 Usability Testing

Redish proposes alternative text examination with usability testing instead of formulas. Usability testing in the field of readability is a method in which representative users work with a text while being observed and documented by trained personnel. The aim is to analyze what readers actually do with a document and which problems they face. Unlike ordinary reading formulas, usability testing allows identifying problems with content, style, word choice, tone, organization, layout, font and others and fixing them.[148]

4.3.4.2 Cloze Procedure

Different from readability formulas that only take into account textual factors, the Cloze procedure aims to predict the understandability of a text based on a measure of comprehension of a sample. Typically, every n^{th} word in a text is deleted and a blank empty space remains. Readers are then asked to predict the correct initial word. This requires understanding context and vocabulary. The procedure therefore depends both on textual and subject factors.[149] *Smith and Taffler* find the correlation between the Flesch index and the Cloze procedure with 0.37 to be relatively low.[150] Nevertheless, this does not per se discredit one of the two concepts.

4.3.4.3 Coh-Metrix

Recent progress in disciplines like computational linguistics, corpus linguistics as well as information extraction and retrieval allows using and analyzing language variables that influence text comprehension in a more fine-grained way than possible with traditional readability formulas. A recent development in this field is the Coh-Metrix developed at the University of Memphis, *"a computational tool that measures cohesion and text difficulty at various levels of language, discourse, and conceptual analysis."*[151] The Coh-Metrix automatically analyzes a range of deep level factors of textual coherence and results in high accuracy.[152] The validity and advantages of the Coh-Metrix already have been proven.[153] It

[148] Redish (2000), pp.132.
[149] Taylor (1953), pp.415.
[150] Smith/Taffler (1992), p.91.
[151] Crossley et al. (2011), p.88.
[152] Graesser (2004), pp.193.
[153] Crossley et al. (2007), p.201.

has also been shown that an adapted L2[154] version provides significantly more accurate results than traditional readability formulas.[155]

4.4 Readability of Corporate Reports

4.4.1 Introduction

Existing literature in the field of examination report readability solely sets the focus on various parts of *annual* reports. Little is known whether *interim* reports during the year have similar characteristics. Moreover, most studies are conducted with samples of annual reports written in English. The following chapters focus on prior research of readability of annual reports and its influencing factors.

4.4.2 Annual Report Readability

4.4.2.1 Pashalian and Crissy (1950)

The first descriptive study on the readability of annual reports that was published in a journal dates back to 1950. *Pashalian and Crissy* examine the readability of companies listed in the Corporate Billion-Dollar Club in 1949. Based on the at that time brand-new Flesch formula, they find that the readability ranges from index 6 to 58 (very difficult to fairly difficult) with an average score of 34.37. Therefore, the reports' reading difficulty is beyond the language experience and fluent comprehension of 75% of the US population. Despite the very small sample size of 26 companies, the difference in Flesch reading score between companies of various industries ranging from 26 (metals and chemicals) to 45 (merchandise) seems striking.[156]

---

[154] second language
[155] Crossley et al. (2011), p.98.
[156] Pashalian/Crissy (1950), pp.244.

4.4.2.2 Soper and Dolphin (1964)

More than a decade after the Flesch index was developed and studies about readability of corporate annual reports were published, *Soper and Dolphin* question if there has been a tendency of improvement in reading ease. They use the same sample as *Pashalian and Crissy* and add corresponding readability data for the year 1961.[157] Average adjusted Flesch readability decreased from 34.2 to 28.8 within 13 years.[158] This difference is significant at the 97% level. Considering potential other factors, the authors conclude unobtrusively:[159]

> *"[...] there has been no over-all improvement in the reading ease."*

Moreover, the authors question the reliability of the Flesch index in assessing the readability of annual reports. They rank text samples both by the readability assessment of independent judges and their ascertaining Flesch index and come to the conclusion that the latter is an appropriate tool for measuring readability. In a next step they compare reading ease and comprehensibility with the help of judges. The higher the annual reports' readability, the higher is the comprehensibility irrespective of other influencing factors.[160] It should be noted that both evaluations are based on very small samples and that they do not eliminate criticism concerning readability formulas.

4.4.2.3 Barnett and Leoffler (1979)

Barnett and Leoffler compare the readability of notes to the financial statements and reports of independent auditors of the first 50 companies of the Fortune's 500 list for the years 1969 and 1975 using the Flesch index. By doing so, they follow the methodology of *Smith and Smith* who conduct a similar study before.[161] *Barnett and Leoffler* find that average readability of the notes decreased significantly from 23.5 to 12.9, a level of extreme difficulty, within six years. Although the readabilities of auditors' reports level at extreme difficulty (negative Flesch index scores), there are significant differences between the respective auditing companies.[162]

[157] one company had to be omitted
[158] Soper/Dolphin (1964), pp.358.
[159] Soper/Dolphin (1964), p.360.
[160] Soper/Dolphin (1964), pp.360.
[161] Barnett/Leoffler (1979), p.51.
[162] Barnett/Leoffler (1979), p.58.

4.4.2.4 Still (1982)

Still examines the readability of 50 chairman's statements in annual reports of UK companies and finds an average Flesch score of 42.5 with a range from 18 to 72. Therefore, a large percentage of the British population would not be able to fluently comprehend the letter.[163]

4.4.3 Studies on Performance Influence on Readability

4.4.3.1 Introduction

The following table provides an overview of research on performance-related factors influencing the readability of corporate annual reports.

Researcher	Year	Sample Size	Report Part	Performance Related Variables	Readability Measure	General Conclusion
Adelberg	1979	16 reports	Management analysis of operations, footnotes, auditor's report	Change in EPS	Cloze procedure	Tendency towards obfuscation of some parts
Courtis	1986	46 and 96 reports	Letter to the shareholders, footnotes	Current ratio, leverage, earnings variability, ROA	Flesch and Fog	No obfuscation
Jones	1988	1 firm, 32 years	Letter to the shareholders	Net profit to sales, ROCE turnover	Flesch	Tendency towards obfuscation
Baker / Kare	1992	44 reports	Letter to the shareholders	Total assets, common shares, ROE, net profit to sales	Flesch	Tendency towards obfuscation

[163] Courtis (1986), p.288.

Smith / Taffler	1992	66 reports	Letter to the shareholders	Failed and non-failed companies, profit, gearing, liquidity, risk	Flesch and Lix	Tendency towards obfuscation
Subramanian / Insley / Blackwell	1993	60 reports	Letter to the shareholders	Improved or worsened profitability	Flesch-Kincaid	Tendency towards obfuscation
Courtis	1995	32 reports (64 firm-years)	Letter to the shareholders, notes	ROI	Flesch, Fog and Lix	No obfuscation
Rutherford	2003	419 reports	Operating and financial report	Turnover, operating profit, profit margin, ROCE; ROE, increase/decrease of EPS, gearing	Flesch	No obfuscation
Smith / Jamil / Johari / Ahmad	2006	513 reports	Letter to the shareholders	Profit, liquidity and gearing	Flesch and BCI	No obfuscation
Li	2008	55,719 firm-years (1993-2003)	Management discussion and analysis, notes	Current earnings, earnings persistence	Fog and length	Tendency towards obfuscation
Hossain / Siddiquee	2008	139 firms	Management discussion	ROA	Flesch and length	limited tendency

			and analysis, notes			towards obfuscation

"letter to the shareholders" also refers to "chairman's statement", "chairman's addresses" etc. The original terms are used in chapters 4.4.3.2 to 4.4.3.12.

EPS = earnings per share, ROA = return on assets, ROCE = return on capital employed, ROE = return on equity, ROI = return on investment, BCI = Bullfighter Composite Index by Deloitte

Table 7: Research studies on the relationship between performance and readability of corporate annual reports (extended and adapted after Jones 1994, p.227. based on the individual studies)

4.4.3.2 Adelberg (1979)

The first study on readability of annual reports, which takes into consideration variables of performance, is conducted by *Adelberg*. From a sample of 16 firms he chooses the management analysis of operations, the footnotes and the auditor's reports. For the non-standard footnotes and the auditor's report he finds that earnings per share (EPS) are indeed related with readability. The higher are EPS, the higher is reading ease. *Adelberg* subsumes that managers underline good results and obfuscate negative results, whether they know it or not.[164]

4.4.3.3 Courtis (1986)

Courtis examines readability of chairmen's addresses and footnotes to financial statements of 46 (1982) and 96 (1983) Canadian annual reports and applies both Flesch and Fog index. His findings concerning readability of the chairman's address are distinct compared to *Still's* study on UK reports ten years prior. Whereas *Still* finds a Flesch index mean of 42.5, *Courtis* finds an average score of around 30.[165]

Besides of these descriptive studies, *Courtis* wants to find out if *"[...] 'negative' readability is positively related to low profitability and high risk"* and *"[...] whether management may have something to hide, and whether it is attempting to achieve this by manipulating the style of written communication."*[166]

The four variables that *Courtis* uses to account for corporate risk and return are current ratio, leverage, earnings variability (standard deviation of annual earnings per share) and return on

[164] Jones (1994), p.226.
[165] Courtis (1986), pp.288.
[166] Courtis (1986), p.291.

assets (ROA). After pursuing a statistical significance test he reasons that there is no relationship between readability and risk or return.[167]

4.4.3.4 Jones (1988)

The research design of *Jones'* study is different in comparison to many others. He conducts a longitudinal study on the chairman's addresses of one company that is analyzed throughout a period of 32 years.[168] Using the Flesch reading ease *Jones* finds a significant downward trend in readability over time. Moreover, he tests potential explanatory factors that influence readability: net profit to sales, ROCE and turnover. Although all factors negatively correlate with readability, only turnover and sales are significant at the 95% and 90% level respectively. Furthermore, the chairman's address has become significantly more difficult to read after the company became listed. This supports the notion that shareholder structure plays a role in determining readability.[169]

4.4.3.5 Baker and Kare (1992)

Baker and Kare conduct a study that examines the influence of firm size (total assets, number of common shares) and profitability (ROE, net profit to sales) on readability of the chairman's address. They find a clear significance for the influence of the ROE at the 95% level. The logarithm of total assets is significant at the 85% level, whereas the two other variables are not significant.[170] *Baker and Kare* confirm the overall low reading ease and reason *"that the managements of more profitable firms tend to be more verbose in their letters to the stockholders"* due to the significantly longer texts of more profitable firms.[171]

4.4.3.6 Smith and Taffler (1992)

Another study that relates performance and readability of chairman's statements is conducted by *Smith and Taffler*. They find the relation between failure and non-failure and readability to be highly significant at the 99.8% level. Moreover, they identify that also liquidity plays a significant role. For gearing they find no relation, whereas risk and profit are significant to mildly significant respectively.[172] They conclude that there is *"a link between clarity of exposition and firm performance."*[173]

---

[167] Courtis (1986), pp.291.
[168] from 1952 to 1985, two years were omitted
[169] Jones (1988), pp.299.
[170] Baker/Kare (1992), pp.1.
[171] Baker/Kare (1992), p.3.
[172] Jones (1994), pp.227.
[173] Smith/Taffler (2000), p.628.

4.4.3.7 Subramanian, Isley and Blackwell (1993)

Selecting 60 US listed companies, dividing them into two equal groups of performance improving and performance worsening and analyzing their letters to the shareholders on readability, *Subramanian et al.* find out that there is a significant relation between performance and readability at the 99.99% level. Moreover, the strength of writing, indicating the simplicity and conciseness, is significantly higher for companies that performed better than the year before.[174]

4.4.3.8 Courtis (1995)

In his second study on the influence of performance on readability, *Courtis* examines 32 Hong Kong public companies in the business years 1986 and 1991. He confirms that their reports are written at a very difficult level that limits fluent comprehension to a minority of the population. Regarding influence of performance on readability, *Courtis* approves his earlier findings that there is no significant relationship.[175]

4.4.3.9 Rutherford (2003)

A considerably sized study on the obfuscation hypothesis is made by *Rutherford*. He tests a broad range of performance-related variables on their influence on reports' readability, but finds no significance.[176] In the light of the size of the study and the big amount of variables tested, *Rutherford* concludes:[177]

"The safest conclusion is that poorly performing entities do not obfuscate their accounting narratives by resorting to textual complexity."

4.4.3.10 Smith, Jamil, Johari and Ahmad (2006)

The work of *Smith et al.* on possible obfuscation of poor results in Malaysian companies is conducted with a sample of 513 reports. They find that readability is neither related with profitability nor with liquidity or gearing. Therefore, their study does not support the obfuscation hypothesis.[178] In fact it even contradicts with some earlier results obtained by *Smith and Taffler.*[179]

---

[174] Subramanian et al. (1993), pp.52.
[175] Courtis (1995), pp.4.
[176] Rutherford (2003), pp.187.
[177] Rutherford (2003), p.204.
[178] Smith et al. (2008), pp.49.
[179] cf. chapter 4.4.3.1

4.4.3.11 Li (2008)

Li conducts a large-scale study on the effect of current earnings and earnings persistence on readability of annual reports by using the Fog index. The sample he uses comprises 55,719 firm-years in total. He bases his assumption that managers have an intention to obfuscate negative results and highlight good results on the Incomplete Revelation Hypothesis (IRH) by *Bloomfield.*[180] *Li* finds that annual reports of firms with poor performance have a statistically significant lower readability. Nevertheless, the impact is economically not relevant. Firms with higher earnings persistence tend to have reports that are easier to read. This effect is also relevant in its economical magnitude.[181]

Moreover, *Li* also qualifies the claim that managers do not intentionally obfuscate since *"[...] negative news is inherently more difficult to present and requires more complicated language"* by finding that the more unexercised stock options managers possess, the greater is the tendency for decreased readability of reports when the persistence of current earnings is low.[182]

Li finally concludes:[183]

> *"[...] the evidence in this paper suggests that managers may be opportunistically structuring the annual reports to hide adverse information from investors."*

4.4.3.12 Hossain/Siddiquee (2008)

Examining the readability of the management discussion and analysis of 139 companies that are listed on the Dhaka Stock Exchange (DSE, Bangladesh) and report in English, *Hossain and Siddiquee* find that average Flesch readability levels at 55.8 (fairly difficult).[184] Compared to other studies, this is a relatively readable average.[185] This could result from the fact that Bengali, not English, represents the official language of Bangladesh.

They find that length of management discussion and readability negatively correlate. Besides of that, they have very slight evidence that performance, measured by return on assets (ROA), and readability describe a co-movement, meaning that both poor and high performing companies report with high readability.[186]

---

[180] Li (2008), pp.222.
[181] Li (2008), p.244.
[182] Li (2008), p.243.
[183] Li (2008), p.245.
[184] Hossain/Siddiquee (2008), pp.6.
[185] cf. chapter 4.4.2
[186] Hossain/Siddiquee (2008), p.11.

4.4.3.13 Conclusio

The dilemma of research on the influence of performance on the readability of corporate (annual) reports appears to be that, despite it has been studied for decades, no final conclusion has yet been found. In 1994 *Jones* notes, *"These results are confused and contradictory."*[187] – It seems that little has changed since then. Interestingly, prior research always focuses on a certain country. No global studies that might reveal more insight have yet been conducted. Since this could be very difficult to realize in a comparable and representative way, every single small study contributes to this still opaque topic.

[187] Jones (1994), p.228.

5. Research Design

5.1 Hypothesis Development

5.1.1 Introduction

This chapter sets out the hypotheses tested in the present study. The hypotheses are based on underlying rationales from existing literature. Based on that, eight hypotheses treating six main topics are developed. It shall be noted beforehand that all hypothesis refer both to German and English language of quarterly reports at FSE. Contradicting results between the two languages lead to a partly acceptance or rejection of a hypothesis.

The underlying research question, as already stated in chapter 1.1, accompanies the process of hypothesis development and is described as follows:

"What influences readability of letters to the shareholders of quarterly reports of publicly listed companies on the Frankfurt Stock Exchange?"

5.1.2 Hypothesis 1 – Level of Difficulty

The very first research in the field of annual report readability by *Pashalian and Crissy* in 1950 provides a clear impression of the very high level of difficulty of company reports. They reason that the majority of the population (75%) is simply not able to read and understand these narratives.[188] Later studies have come to very similar conclusions.[189] Accounting scandals in the new millennium and the following Sarbanes-Oxley Act have further decreased the level of readability of reports.[190] Nevertheless, previous studies almost exclusively focus on *annual* reports of Anglo-American companies. Especially German or German/English reports have not yet been deeply researched in this respect. *Hossain and Siddiquee* show that for bilingual reports in Bangladesh, where English is not the first language, the level of (English) reports' readability is higher than in the Anglo-American market.[191]

In the light of the international orientation of the companies on the Prime Market of FSE it is reasonable to expect that letters to shareholders of its companies are also written at a considerable level of difficulty. Possession of shares is often regarded as elite and therefore reserved to educated categories that are eager and able to read difficult texts.

---

[188] Pashalian/Crissy (1950), pp.244.
[189] Soper/Dolphin (1964), Barnett/Leoffler (1979), Courtis (1986), Courtis (1995), Li (2008) and others
[190] Dempsey et al. (2012), p.468.
[191] Hossain/Siddiquee (2008), pp.1.

Hypothesis 1.1:

The readability of letters to the shareholders of quarterly reports is at a level that is commonly considered to be at least "difficult".

Furthermore, it has to be questioned whether the readability of the reports has the same level irrespective of the industry which the companies belong to. *Courtis* denies any significant difference, but has to confess a relatively small sample.[192] In contrast to that, a recent study by *Lehavy et al.* shows that there is significant difference among industries for SEC-listed companies.[193] Still, the magnitude seems to be rather small. It is conceivable that a similar scenario is existent for companies listed on FSE.

Companies should use different types of vocabulary depending on the industry that they operate in. Moreover, it is also likely that industries attract certain kinds of shareholders that demand specific levels of readability. These potential trends should be visible when it comes to readability of letters to the shareholders.

Hypothesis 1.2:

The readability of letters to the shareholders of quarterly reports varies between different industries.

5.1.3 Hypothesis 2 – Bilingual Reports

In the Prime Market of FSE all companies, with exceptions mentioned in chapter 2.4.3, have to provide bilingual reports in German and English. It is yet very unclear how the levels of readability in different languages of the same company relate to each other. Two studies that potentially could have researched and answered this question, *Mohamad and Rahman* (2006) and *Hossain and Siddiquee* (2008), failed to do so.

The content of a letter to the shareholders of one company equals to a very wide extent, irrespective of what language is used. Consequently, the usage of firm-specific technical vocabulary resembles within a company independent of the language. Moreover, German and English have similarities in grammar and word structure. A difficult sentence in German can be expected to be rather difficult in English as well, if correctly translated. Most importantly, already mentioned factors like performance and earnings persistency are said to influence the level of readability.[194] If this and the influence of potential other factors hold true, then there

---

[192] Courtis (1995), p.10.

[193] Lehavy et al. (2011), pp.1093.

[194] cf. chapter 4.4.3

is strong evidence that the effect should be visible for both types of languages. A correlation between the readability levels of the languages would be the result.

Hypothesis 2:

In bilingual reports, there is a linear correlation between the readability levels in German and English.

5.1.4 Hypothesis 3 – Company Size

Various studies in the field of readability include company size in their analysis as a control variable. While *Courtis* assumes a positive relation between size and readability, *Li* hypothesizes larger firms to publish reports that are more complex. *Courtis* does not find any significant relationship. *Li* finds a high influence for the notes to the financial statements. For the management discussion he finds no significance.[195] *Li's* results are indeed explicable: Bigger firms have higher accounting and disclosure requirements. These texts are often standardized and of higher difficulty and thus result in a lower reading ease of the overall report. Nevertheless, the present study solely focuses on letters to the shareholders, a fact which heavily diminishes the influence of the findings of *Li*. A study conducted by *Baker and Kare* shows a significant positive link at the 85% level between the logarithm of the dollar amount of the total assets and the reading ease of letters to the shareholders. In their view big companies are confronted with strong investment communities that desire and claim readable reports. Moreover, the bigger a firm is, the bigger are the potential resources that can be used to present simple and effective reports. Nevertheless, in the light of the very small sample of 44 companies and the age of the study, it has to be questioned if their results still have validity.[196]

Due to the controversial and still uncertain previous studies, one should also keep the option in mind that there is simply no relevant relation between company size and readability. The explanatory value of such a general variable has to be questioned.

Hypothesis 3:

The readability of letters to the shareholders of quarterly reports is not dependent on company size.

---

[195] Courtis (1995), pp.9. and Li (2008), pp.230.

[196] Baker/Kare (1992), pp.2.

5.1.5 Hypothesis 4 – Shareholder Independence

Yet, including shareholder independence in readability studies is an unknown concept, but chapter 3.5.3 provides enough reasons to assume an influence.

The underlying premise in this study is that every company's management has a certain degree of independence from its shareholders. A typical attempt to quantify this degree is to analyze the shareholder structure and the power constellations. It provides information on how much controlling influence can be expected to be exerted by shareholders. Controlling influence can potentially also mean that shareholders urge the management to transmit all relevant information in their agency relationship in an easy and understandable way. It can be anticipated that shareholders prefer readable over less readable reports since readability has an influence on the information processing costs that are desired to be minimal.

Hypothesis 4:

The readability of letters to the shareholders in quarterly reports depends on the independence of the management from the shareholders.

5.1.6 Hypothesis 5 – Share Price Volatility

The broad concept of risk has already been discussed in some studies. *Courtis* uses the variability of earnings as a proxy for risk, but cannot find any significant relationship between this measure and readability.[197] However, *Li* uses a similar variable, calculated as the standard deviation of operating earnings, and shows a clearly significant negative relationship to the readability of the management discussion and the annual report as a whole. Moreover, he also uses a more capital market oriented approach to assess the risk of a business by considering the standard deviation of monthly stock returns. This measure is negatively correlated with readability at the 99% level.[198]

Similar to the underlying assumptions about management obfuscation of negative results, it is cogitable that managers attempt to conceal high risk, be it positive or negative, by adjusting the level of readability of letters to the shareholders. Especially due to the recent turbulences on global stock exchanges this intention can be of high interest. Companies having a steady share price are probably more preferred by investors that are no experts and do not want to be confronted with permanent buy, sell or hold decisions. Consequently, they should seek for easy to process, readable information. On the other hand, traders with a high knowledge could

[197] Courtis (1986), pp.291.
[198] Li (2008), pp.231.

accept that share price volatility, which also offers potential gains, is connected with information that is difficult to process.

Hypothesis 5:

The readability of letters to the shareholders in quarterly reports depends on share price volatility.

5.1.7 Hypothesis 6 – Financial Performance

The most elemental question of this study is whether there is a link between company performance and readability of the letter to the shareholders. As already extensively discussed in chapter 4.4.3, there is yet no conclusive answer for this question. So far the results are even heavily contradicting each other. Also it is not clear whether revenue and profit have the same influence. This situation perhaps can be attributed to different samples, variables and measurement methods.

The potential link between low performance and low readability grounds on the following considerations: Firstly, low performance is usually seen as poor work of the management. Managers therefore should have an incentive to avert standing in the spotlight of the investors' community. One potential way to do this, besides others, is to adjust the style of communication in their reports. This does not inherently mean that managers tend to spread lies when results are poor. Rather they *"make it more difficult for investors to uncover information that the managers do not want uncovered"*.[199] Secondly, poor results could also require more explanatory effort that results in longer sentences and more complex words. Nevertheless, this possible reason, which would speak against intentional obfuscation, has already been denied by *Li*.[200]

Hypothesis 6.1:

The readability of letters to the shareholders in quarterly reports depends on profit margins.

Hypothesis 6.2:

The readability of letters to the shareholders in quarterly reports depends on revenues.

[199] Li (2008), p.224.
[200] Li (2008), p.243.

5.2 Methodology

5.2.1 Research Objects

Although readability studies on company reports have quite a long history, there is still no mutual understanding amongst researches which part of a report is suitable to be examined.[201] A very rough classification could be drawn by separating reports into letter to the shareholders, management discussion, notes to the financial statements and auditor's report.

The reasons for focusing on the letters to the shareholders as an object of research mentioned by *Subramanian et al.* are convincing and also decisive for this study: A letter to the shareholders is typically a message by the board or its chairman which reviews the company's activities and results of the previous period. Relevant topics have to be treated within very limited scale. Moreover, it often offers an outlook and future projections.[202] For investors it forms a basis for investment decisions since this section forms the most widely read one.[203] Additionally, letters to the shareholders are not as technical as the financial statements.[204] This brings the advantage that automated analysis can be applied more easily.

More specifically, it is the letters to the shareholders of quarterly reports of companies that are listed on the Prime Market on FSE which form the object of research in this study. Quarterly reports have not yet been considered in any of the previous studies on readability. It is therefore unclear whether and how they react to different company related variables. Companies on FSE also have not yet been examined in the field of readability studies.

5.2.2 Sample

The underlying sample for this study is based on the business research database Orbis which integrates the European database Amadeus and the database Zephyr. Most importantly for this study, Orbis offers a detailed range of capital market, reporting and property information for FSE-listed companies that can be easily extracted as a Microsoft Excel file and then processed further.

The raw format of this file, exported on 04.02.2013, includes 578 datasets from companies listed on FSE that consist, amongst secondary, of the following main variables:

---

[201] cf. chapter 4.4.3.1

[202] Subramanian et al. (1993), p.53.

[203] Balata (2005), p.5.

[204] Subramanian et al. (1993), p.53.

- Company number
- Company name
- ISIN code
- NACE main section
- Number of employees, year end 2009
- Total assets, year end 2009
- BvDEP Independence Indicator, per 04.02.2013[205]
- Share price, year-end 2007-2011 (if available)
- Revenue, year-end 2008-2009
- Profit margin, year-end 2008-2009

A database with the pdf-files of all quarterly reports of 2009 of the Prime Market of FSE was then used to receive information on the readability of the letters to the shareholders of the respective companies. Only the third quarter reports were processed since they tend to have the biggest predictive quality on the whole business year's results and thus can be regarded as most influential on shareholders' investment decisions. *Jordan* refers to third quarter reports as *"harbinger of the annual report"* in respect to timing and content.[206] Those companies that did not provide a letter to the shareholders or a very similar type of narrative were omitted from the database. Also those companies that did not report bilingually were not considered.
The process of extracting the letter to the shareholders was aggravated by the fact that all pdf-files locked the text copy function through a password. This obstacle was cleared with the help of software that allows automated unlocking of pdf-files.[207] For obtaining a precise and comparable readability scores, the free online software Readbility-score.com was used.[208] Compared to other providers of readability scores, it proved to have a very high level of efficiency and reliability. Although a broad range of indices is automatically calculated, only the Flesch score was used for the sample.[209] Independent of the disadvantage of limited comparability with verbal difficulty charts, it is also reasonable to use the Flesch formula for German reports to have a common data basis.

[205] Unfortunately, this information was only available for the latest reference date. Yet it represents a useful approximation.
[206] Jordan (1973), p.616.
[207] Wondershare PDF Password Remover
[208] Readability-score.com (2013)
[209] cf. chapter 4.2.6

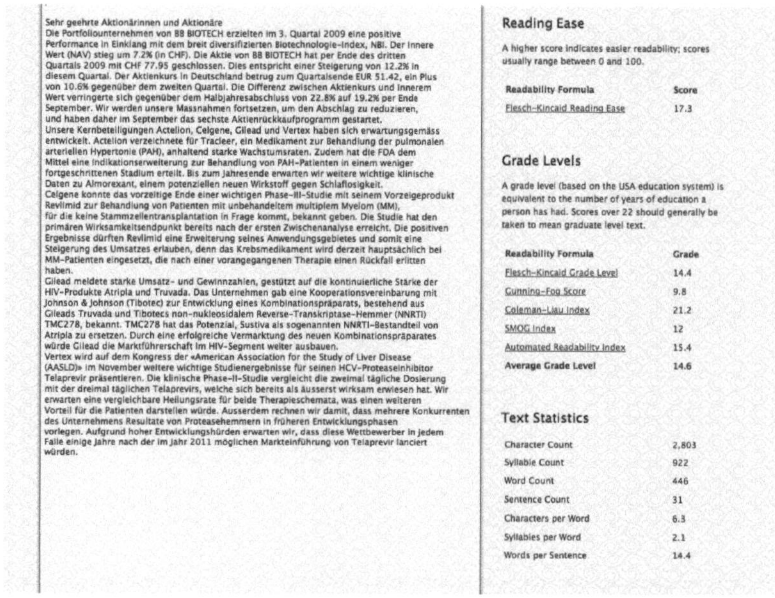

Sehr geehrte Aktionärinnen und Aktionäre
Die Portfoliounternehmen von BB BIOTECH erzielten im 3. Quartal 2009 eine positive Performance in Einklang mit dem breit diversifizierten Biotechnologie-Index, NBI. Der Innere Wert (NAV) stieg um 7.2% (in CHF). Die Aktie von BB BIOTECH hat per Ende des dritten Quartals 2009 mit CHF 77.95 geschlossen. Dies entspricht einer Steigerung von 12.2% in diesem Quartal. Der Aktienkurs in Deutschland betrug zum Quartalsende EUR 51.42, ein Plus von 10.6% gegenüber dem zweiten Quartal. Die Differenz zwischen Aktienkurs und Innerem Wert verringerte sich gegenüber dem Halbjahresabschluss von 22.8% auf 19.2% per Ende September. Wir werden unsere Massnahmen fortsetzen, um den Abschlag zu reduzieren, und haben daher im September das sechste Aktienrückkaufprogramm gestartet.
Unsere Kernbeteiligungen Actelion, Celgene, Gilead und Vertex haben sich erwartungsgemäss entwickelt. Actelion verzeichnete für Tracleer, ein Medikament zur Behandlung der pulmonalen arteriellen Hypertonie (PAH), anhaltend starke Wachstumsraten. Zudem hat die FDA dem Mittel eine Indikationserweiterung zur Behandlung von PAH-Patienten in einem weniger fortgeschrittenen Stadium erteilt. Bis zum Jahresende erwarten wir weitere wichtige klinische Daten zu Almorexant, einem potenziellen neuen Wirkstoff gegen Schlaflosigkeit.
Celgene konnte das vorzeitige Ende einer wichtigen Phase-III-Studie mit seinem Vorzeigeprodukt Revlimid zur Behandlung von Patienten mit unbehandeltem multiplem Myelom (MM), für die keine Stammzellentransplantation in Frage kommt, bekannt geben. Die Studie hat den primären Wirksamkeitsendpunkt bereits nach der ersten Zwischenanalyse erreicht. Die positiven Ergebnisse dürften Revlimid eine Erweiterung seines Anwendungsgebietes und somit eine Steigerung des Umsatzes erlauben, denn das Krebsmedikament wird derzeit hauptsächlich bei MM-Patienten eingesetzt, die nach einer vorangegangenen Therapie einen Rückfall erlitten haben.
Gilead meldete starke Umsatz- und Gewinnzahlen, gestützt auf die kontinuierliche Stärke der HIV-Produkte Atripla und Truvada. Das Unternehmen gab eine Kooperationsvereinbarung mit Johnson & Johnson (Tibotec) zur Entwicklung eines Kombinationspräparats, bestehend aus Gileads Truvada und Tibotecs non-nukleosidalem Reverse-Transkriptase-Hemmer (NNRTI) TMC278, bekannt. TMC278 hat das Potenzial, Sustiva als sogenannten NNRTI-Bestandteil von Atripla zu ersetzen. Durch eine erfolgreiche Vermarktung des neuen Kombinationspräparates würde Gilead die Marktführerschaft im HIV-Segment weiter ausbauen.
Vertex wird auf dem Kongress der «American Association for the Study of Liver Disease (AASLD)» im November weitere wichtige Studienergebnisse für seinen HCV-Proteaseinhibitor Telaprevir präsentieren. Die klinische Phase-II-Studie vergleicht die zweimal tägliche Dosierung mit der dreimal täglichen Telaprevirs, welche sich bereits als äusserst wirksam erwiesen hat. Wir erwarten eine vergleichbare Heilungsrate für beide Therapieschemata, was einen weiteren Vorteil für die Patienten darstellen würde. Ausserdem rechnen wir damit, dass mehrere Konkurrenten des Unternehmens Resultate von Proteasehemmern in früheren Entwicklungsphasen vorlegen. Aufgrund hoher Entwicklungshürden erwarten wir, dass diese Wettbewerber in jedem Falle einige Jahre nach der im Jahr 2011 möglichen Markteinführung von Telaprevir lanciert würden.

Reading Ease

A higher score indicates easier readability; scores usually range between 0 and 100.

Readability Formula	Score
Flesch-Kincaid Reading Ease	17.3

Grade Levels

A grade level (based on the USA education system) is equivalent to the number of years of education a person has had. Scores over 22 should generally be taken to mean graduate level text.

Readability Formula	Grade
Flesch-Kincaid Grade Level	14.4
Gunning-Fog Score	9.8
Coleman-Liau Index	21.2
SMOG Index	12
Automated Readability Index	15.4
Average Grade Level	14.6

Text Statistics

Character Count	2,803
Syllable Count	922
Word Count	446
Sentence Count	31
Characters per Word	6.3
Syllables per Word	2.1
Words per Sentence	14.4

Figure 6: Readability-score.com analysis form (Readability-score.com 2013)

A substantial disadvantage of business-related texts in readability research, which is hardly mentioned in existing literature and therefore causes concern, is the fact that some companies tend to use a broad range of abbreviations and decimal places. Since most readability formulas depend on the length of sentences and automated index generators that count every dot as the end of such, the outcome of such an analysis can be seriously distorted. Therefore, altogether four readability scores were collected for each company: Firstly, a raw score which does not consider the issue of irrelevant dots for German and English. Secondly, an adjusted score which only counts sentences that are also perceived as such by the reader in both German and English. To account for the superfluous dots, the extracts from third quarter reports were manually reviewed and adjusted correspondingly. These adjustments are also in line with the original thoughts of *Flesch: "In counting sentences, I follow the units of thought rather than the punctuation".*[210] The following example shall demonstrate how severe the mentioned problem is:

[210] Flesch (1948), pp.227.

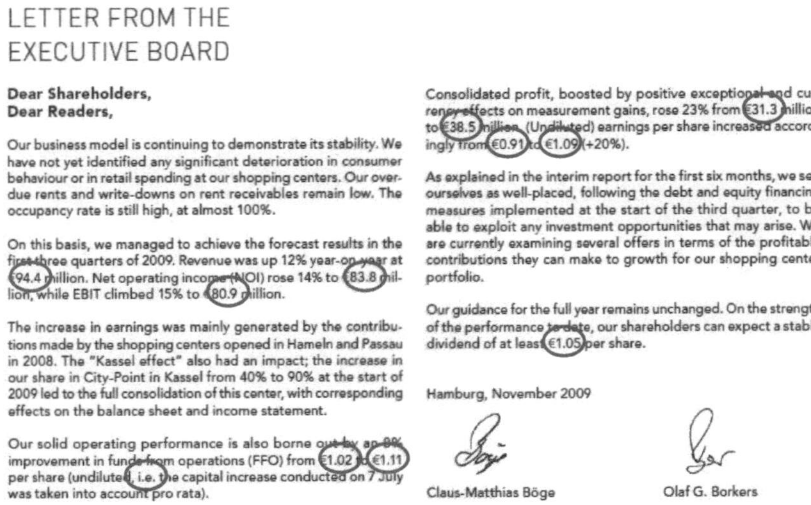
LETTER FROM THE
EXECUTIVE BOARD

Dear Shareholders,
Dear Readers,

Our business model is continuing to demonstrate its stability. We have not yet identified any significant deterioration in consumer behaviour or in retail spending at our shopping centers. Our overdue rents and write-downs on rent receivables remain low. The occupancy rate is still high, at almost 100%.

On this basis, we managed to achieve the forecast results in the first three quarters of 2009. Revenue was up 12% year-on-year at €94.4 million. Net operating income (NOI) rose 14% to €83.8 million, while EBIT climbed 15% to €80.9 million.

The increase in earnings was mainly generated by the contributions made by the shopping centers opened in Hameln and Passau in 2008. The "Kassel effect" also had an impact; the increase in our share in City-Point in Kassel from 40% to 90% at the start of 2009 led to the full consolidation of this center, with corresponding effects on the balance sheet and income statement.

Our solid operating performance is also borne out by an 8% improvement in funds from operations (FFO) from €1.02 to €1.11 per share (undiluted, i.e. the capital increase conducted on 7 July was taken into account pro rata).

Consolidated profit, boosted by positive exceptional and currency effects on measurement gains, rose 23% from €31.3 million to €38.5 million. (Undiluted) earnings per share increased accordingly from €0.91 to €1.09 (+20%).

As explained in the interim report for the first six months, we see ourselves as well-placed, following the debt and equity financing measures implemented at the start of the third quarter, to be able to exploit any investment opportunities that may arise. We are currently examining several offers in terms of the profitable contributions they can make to growth for our shopping center portfolio.

Our guidance for the full year remains unchanged. On the strength of the performance to date, our shareholders can expect a stable dividend of at least €1.05 per share.

Hamburg, November 2009

Claus-Matthias Böge   Olaf G. Borkers

Figure 7: Superfluous dots in a letter to the shareholders (Deutsche Euroshop AG 2009, p.1.)

For this English letter to the shareholders, the unadjusted Flesch raw score is 58.9. Considering the fact that not every dot in the text means the end of a sentence, the adjusted Flesch score is 48.8.

Furthermore, rules had to be set up to assure that the letters to the shareholders were treated similarly in the process of analysis. Headlines that were not directly part of the letter and the signatures of the board members were not considered. The complementary closure was seen as part of the letter and therefore influenced the readability score. All pictures and graphs, if any, were also ignored. Although *Flesch* originally proposes to draw 100-word samples, the whole letters to the shareholders were analyzed. In the light of their small size, this modification seems to be reasonable.[211]

The resulting sample contains 104 companies plus their main variables and four readability scores. All data are complete with the exception of occasional vacancies for year-end share prices, which do not represent a severe problem in further data analysis.

5.2.3 Statistical Methods

The main statistical methods that are applied to analyze the sample and the formulated hypotheses are histogram, t-test, correlation analysis and multiple regression analysis. Moreover, basic statistical concepts like mean, standard deviation, kurtosis and skewness are

[211] cf. chapter 4.2.6.

used for the descriptive summary statistics. A (significant) relation or difference is generally determined with the help of the 95% significance level. Still, this does not represent a sharp cutting line, but rather a reference point for interpretational purpose.

The analysis of data is entirely carried out with the help of the data analysis functions in Microsoft Excel. To account for the conventional usage of kurtosis in statistics, the Microsoft Excel value is adjusted by adding 3.

6. Results

6.1 Descriptive Statistics

6.1.1 Introduction

This chapter aims to familiarize the reader with key parameters of the sample and attempts to give an understanding of the order of magnitude of the data. Later, the obtained data form the basis of the (in)dependent variables in multiple regression analyses.

6.1.2 Main Variables

Table 8 shows key statistical parameters of the independent variables from the sample. Most variables differ distinctly from a normal distribution with skewness of 0 and kurtosis of 3.

A standard deviation that exceeds the mean and high values for both kurtosis and skewness for the number of employees indicate a leptokurtic distribution with extreme values on the right (positive) side. A very similar situation may be observed for the total assets and the operating revenues. Since there is strong notion that a linear model of the variables employees and total assets is not useful for the multiple regression analysis, the natural logarithm is calculated and used instead. This conversion is not necessary for the operating revenues since they are only transformed into improved (1) and not-improved (0) dummy variables.

The average BvDEP Independence Indicator levels slightly above 2. Since a transformation of its categories in letters into numbers has been pursued before, the explanatory power of this figure is heavily limited.[212]

Average profit margins are single-digit and decreased between 2008 and 2009. Only 42% of the observed firms could improve their margins. The magnitude of the standard deviations of the profit margins clearly outweighs their means. This partly comes from the fact that profit margins can have both positive and negative values. On average, the operating revenues also decreased. The high standard deviations in comparison to the means result from the non-normal, leptokurtic distribution with extreme positive values.

The average share price development of the sample exemplary catches the picture of German and global stock exchanges prior, during and after the financial crisis.

[212] cf. chapter 3.5.3, A=1, B=2, C=3 and D=4, no occurrence of type U

Variable	Year	Mean	Standard Deviation	Skewness	Kurtosis
Employees	2009	10,450	44,830	8.04	75.43
Total assets (in th. EUR)	2009	4,218,767	18,143,711	6.70	52.20
BvDEP Independence Indicator	2013	2.09	1.16	0.71	- 3.97
Profit margin (in %)	2008	4.10	20.56	- 0.56	9.25
	2009	2.29	17.24	- 1.25	8.13
Profit margin increase	2008/09	0.42	0.50	0.32	- 4.94
Operating revenue (in th. EUR)	2008	3,335,423	12,119,328	5.49	37.96
	2009	3,158,690	11,843,914	5.87	42.53
Operating revenue increase	2008/09	0.39	0.49	0.44	- 4.84
Share price (in EUR)	2007	25.81	35.85	3.18	14.35
	2008	11.59	14.40	2.70	11.65
	2009	14.80	18.12	3.02	15.39
	2010	17.59	20.92	2.78	13.15
	2011	14.22	15.17	1.94	7.09
Share price volatility	2007-11	0.45	0.28	2.38	12.46

All figures refer to the last day of the year, except of "Ir

Profit margin/Operating revenue increase: "1" means in

Share price volatility = standard deviation of share pric€

n=104

Table 8: Descriptive statistics of the sample

6.1.3 Readability Scores

6.1.3.1 Adjusted Flesch Score in German

The distribution of the 104 values of adjusted Flesch scores in German is slightly skewed to the right and leptokurtic. With a minimum Flesch value of 2.50 and a maximum of 48.60, the sample contains a broad spectrum of different levels of readability.

Summary Statistics Adjusted Flesch Score in German	
Mean	21.72
Standard Error	0.84
Median	23.10
Mode	15.90
Standard Deviation	8.53
Sample Variance	72.78
Kurtosis	3.23
Skewness	0.12
Range	46.10
Minimum	2.50
Maximum	48.60
Sum	2259.20
Number of Observations	104
Confidence level (95.0%)	1.66

Table 9: Summary statistics adjusted Flesch score in German

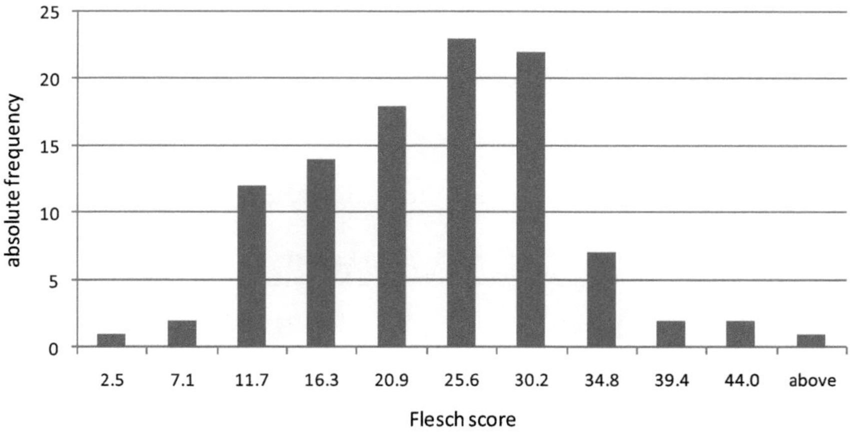

Figure 8: Distribution adjusted Flesch score in German

6.1.3.2 Adjusted Flesch Score in English

With an average adjusted Flesch score in English of 43.24 a clear difference to the German counterpart is noticeable. Although the languages are related, this effect is unsurprising since the languages have distinct styles of expression. The observed values range from Flesch score 25.00 to 66.50.

Summary Statistics Adjusted Flesch Score in English	
Mean	43.24
Standard Error	0.68
Median	43.15
Mode	46.00
Standard Deviation	6.91
Sample Variance	47.70
Kurtosis	3.79
Skewness	0.03
Range	41.50
Minimum	25.00
Maximum	66.50
Sum	4497.30
Number of Observations	104.00
Confidence level (95.0%)	1.34

Table 10: Summary statistics adjusted Flesch score in English

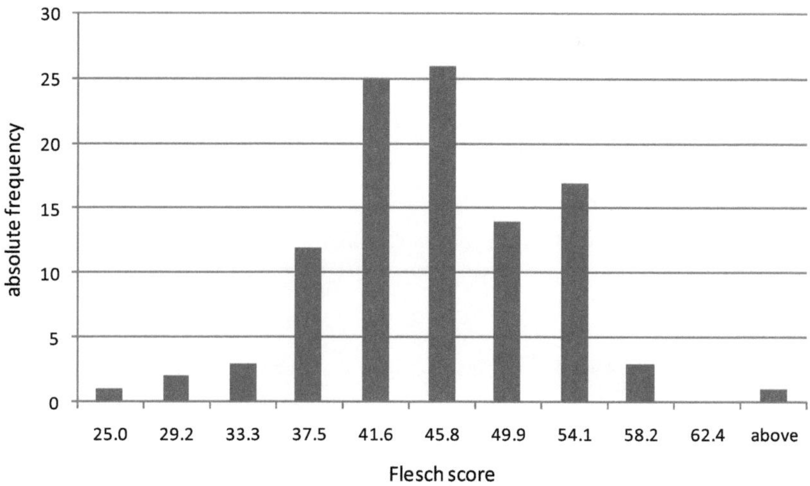

Figure 9: Distribution adjusted Flesch score in English

6.1.3.3 Raw Flesch Score in German

The average raw Flesch score in German is higher than the average adjusted Flesch score.[213] A nearly bell-shaped distribution can be observed with values between 2.50 and 53.90.

Summary Statistics Raw Flesch Score in German	
Mean	26.47
Standard Error	0.96
Median	26.95
Mode	31.50
Standard Deviation	9.74
Sample Variance	94.96
Kurtosis	3.20
Skewness	0.01
Range	51.40
Minimum	2.50
Maximum	53.90
Sum	2753.30
Number of Observations	104.00
Confidence level (95.0%)	1.90

Table 11: Summary statistics raw Flesch score in German

213 cf. chapter 5.2.2

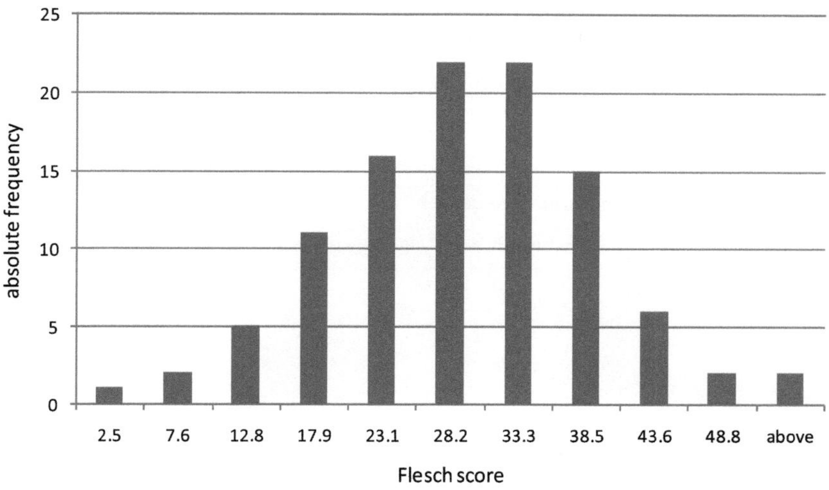

Figure 10: Distribution raw Flesch score in German

6.1.3.4 Raw Flesch Score in English

Also for the raw Flesch score in English the values are higher than for the adjusted score. The sample values range between 25.60 and 69.30.

Summary Statistics **Raw Flesch Score in English**	
Mean	48.13
Standard Error	0.79
Median	48.30
Mode	48.20
Standard Deviation	8.06
Sample Variance	64.99
Kurtosis	3.40
Skewness	0.00
Range	43.70
Minimum	25.60
Maximum	69.30
Sum	5005.20
Number of Observations	104.00
Confidence level (95.0%)	1.57

Table 12: Summary statistics raw Flesch score in English

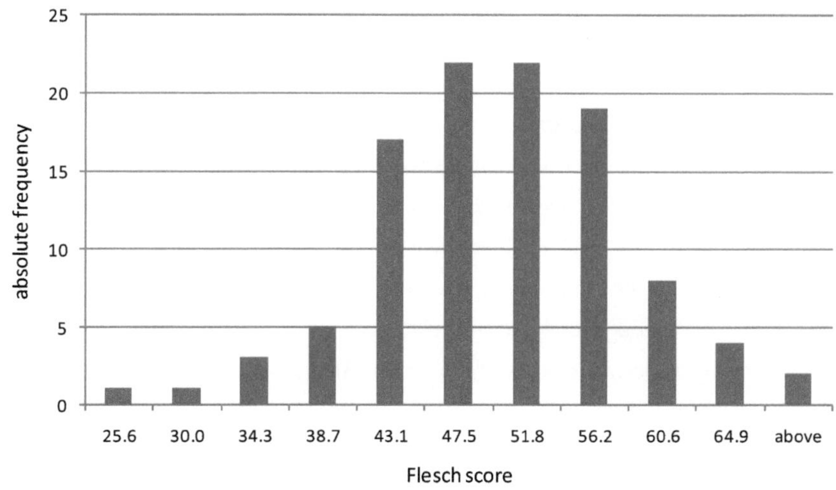

Figure 11: Distribution raw Flesch score in English

6.2 Hypothesis Testing

6.2.1 Introduction

Due to the fact that different readability scores have been ascertained, it is necessary to determine which variables have primary explanatory impact during the testing process of the hypotheses. In general, adjusted readability scores are of prime importance since they are conceptually more developed. If the results for German and English are not in line, the option of partly accepting or rejecting a hypothesis remains. Occasionally it may also be valuable to compare results with unadjusted, raw readability scores. This defined procedure allows for reducing complexity in the testing process.

6.2.2 Testing Hypothesis 1 – Level of Difficulty

6.2.2.1 Testing Hypothesis 1.1

Comparing the Flesch difficulty classification in Table 5 and the average adjusted Flesch score in English of 43.24 obtained from the sample, the letters to the shareholders have a readability level that can be described as "difficult" and representative for academic literature. This is assumed to be the case for Flesch scores between 30 and 50.

Since the estimated mean very likely differs from the population mean, a confidence interval that considers estimated mean, standard deviation and sample size is calculated. The actual average lies within the interval [41.92, 44.57] with 95% probability and within the interval [41.50, 44.99] with 99% probability. Hence, this fulfills the needs to be classified as "difficult".

Hypothesis 1.1 is therefore **accepted** for the English letters to the reports.

For the average adjusted Flesch score in German it is not expedient to compare the results with a classification table that is based on English empirical values only. Nevertheless, with an estimated mean of 21.72 and confidence intervals of [20.08, 23.36] with 95% probability and [19.56, 23.88] with 99% probability, it is very likely, yet unconfirmed, that the readability could also be classified at least as "difficult". Since there is no *academic* approach yet to convert the results tables, it is necessary to refrain from answering hypothesis 1.1 for the German reports from a methodological point of view.[214]

6.2.2.2 Testing Hypothesis 1.2

Testing a hypothesis based on industry specifics is often a problematic procedure since the initial sample size is split into fractions of small size. This is also the case in the present study. The subsamples vary between one (mining, quarrying and construction) and 37 (manufacturing) in their respective size. To account for the limited representative function of very small subsamples, only those with a minimum size of five scores are processed further. For the remaining seven categories confidence intervals are then calculated and matched with each other in both languages. The analysis in Table 14 shows that none of the combinations indicates a statistically significant difference between two categories.

Hypothesis 1.2 is therefore **rejected.**

NACE Rev. 2 main section	Size Subsample	Mean German	Standard Deviation German	Mean English	Standard Deviatio n English
B - Mining and quarrying	1	33.5	n.a	53.9	n.a
C - Manufacturing	*37*	*22.16*	*8.83*	*43.36*	*7.32*
D - Electricity, gas, steam and air conditioning supply	*7*	*24.24*	*5.56*	*45.07*	*4.71*
F - Construction	1	21.1	n.a	40.7	n.a
G - Wholesale and retail trade; repair of motor	*10*	*20.41*	*7.06*	*42.49*	*4.73*

[214] The authors of Leichtlesbar.ch propose to shift down the English language classification by a score of 20 points to have a basis of comparison.

vehicles and motorcycles					
H - Transportation and storage	*5*	*19.68*	*14.19*	*44.78*	*9.16*
J - Information and communication	*22*	*22.2*	*8.59*	*43.8*	*6.6*
K - Financial and insurance activities	2	22.1	8.77	42.6	11.17
L - Real estate activities	*7*	*17.74*	*7.29*	*39.39*	*7.63*
M - Professional, scientific and technical activities	*6*	*20.42*	*11.55*	*41.52*	*9.52*
Q - Human health and social work activities	2	20.85	7.99	41.95	10.39
S - Other service activities	4	22.85	8.47	44.18	4.61

Table 13: Readability by industries

	Adjusted Flesch Score German						
	C	D	G	H	J	L	M
	19.31 - 24.99	20.12 - 28.34	16.03 - 24.76	7.24 - 32.05	18.61 - 25.77	12.34 - 23.11	11.18 - 29.61
C	-	no	no	no	no	no	no
D	no	-	no	no	no	no	no
G	no	no	-	no	no	no	no
H	no	no	no	-	no	no	no
J	no	no	no	no	-	no	no
L	no	no	no	no	no	-	no
M	no	no	no	no	no	no	-

	Adjusted Flesch Score English						
	C	D	G	H	J	**L**	M
	41.00 - 45.71	41.58 - 48.54	39.56 - 45.41	36.75 - 52.77	41.04 - 46.54	33.74 - 45.01	33.90 - 49.10
C	-	no	no	no	no	no	no
D	no	-	no	no	no	no	no

G	no	no	-	no	no	no	no
H	no	no	no	-	no	no	no
J	no	no	no	no	-	no	no
L	no	no	no	no	no	-	no
M	no	no	no	no	no	no	-

no = no significant difference between two industries

Table 14: Test on industry difference with confidence intervals

6.2.3 Testing Hypothesis 2 – Bilingual Reports

Hypothesis 2 is tested based on a linear correlation analysis, which explains whether a relationship between two variables exists.

Figure 12 shows a visible positive relationship between the adjusted English Flesch score and the adjusted German Flesch score with R^2=0.55. A statement whether one variable depends on the other cannot be provided.

Hypothesis 2 is therefore **accepted.**

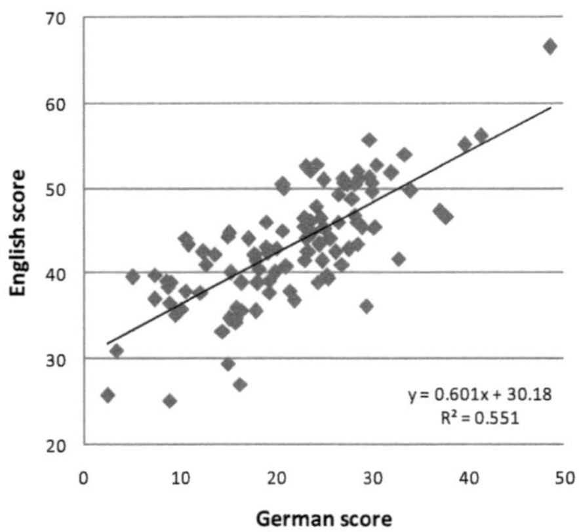

Figure 12: Readability correlation in bilingual quarterly reports

6.2.4 Testing Hypothesis 3 – Company Size

For answering the following hypotheses, including company size, multiple regression analyses with Flesch scores for both languages as dependent variables are pursued (Tables 15 and 16). Also the multiple regression analyses with raw Flesch scores are provided and referred to if necessary (Tables 17 and 18). The tables in this chapter are also relevant for hypotheses 4 to 6 and will not be illustrated again.

Two popular variables are used as indicators for company size: employees and total assets. Both variables are transformed using natural logarithms (ln) to account for the expected non-linear relationship in the regression.

While for the German letters to the shareholders a positive influence of the number of employees on readability can be observed, the opposite is the case for the total assets. For the English reports both variables have a positive influence on the readability score. Nevertheless, the very high p-values indicate that these relationships are not significant. Also the regressions based on raw Flesch scores show no significant relationships in respect to company size.

Hypothesis 3 is therefore **accepted.**

Regression Statistics	
Multiple R	0.234
R Square	0.055
Adjusted R Sq.	-0.004
Standard Error	8.547
Observations	104

ANOVA

	Degrees of Freedom	*Square (SS)*	*Sums Mean Square Sum (MS)*	*F*	*Significance F*
Regression	6	410.470	68.412	0.936	0.473
Residue	97	7086.075	73.052		
Total	103	7496.545			

	Coefficients	*Standard Error*	*t Stat*	*P-value*	*Lower 95%*	*Upper 95%*
Intercept	16.516	6.472	2.552	0.012	3.670	29.361
ln Employees	0.374	0.597	0.626	0.533	-0.812	1.559
ln Total Assets	-0.077	0.615	-0.126	0.900	-1.297	1.143
BvDEP Independence Ind.	0.907	0.785	1.154	0.251	-0.652	2.465
Share Price Volatility	-0.454	3.079	-0.148	0.883	-6.565	5.656
Profit Margin Increase	3.038	1.758	1.727	0.087	-0.452	6.528
Revenue Increase	1.652	1.818	0.908	0.366	-1.957	5.260

Table 15: Regression analysis adjusted Flesch score German

Regression Statistics	
Multiple R	0.162
R Square	0.026
Adjusted R Sq.	-0.034
Standard Error	7.023
Observations	104

ANOVA

	Degrees of Freedom	*Square Sums (SS)*	*Mean Square Sum (MS)*	*F*	*Significance F*
Regression	6	128.355	21.393	0.434	0.855
Residue	97	4784.340	49.323		
Total	103	4912.695			

	Coefficients	*Standard Error*	*t Stat*	*P-value*	*Lower 95%*	*Upper 95%*
Intercept	39.387	5.318	7.406	0.000	28.832	49.942
ln Employees	0.490	0.491	0.999	0.320	-0.484	1.465
ln Total Assets	0.032	0.505	0.064	0.949	-0.970	1.035
BvDEP Independence Indicator	0.072	0.645	0.111	0.912	-1.209	1.353
Share Price Volatility	-0.913	2.530	-0.361	0.719	-5.934	4.108
Profit Margin Increase	0.078	1.445	0.054	0.957	-2.790	2.946
Revenue Increase	0.779	1.494	0.521	0.603	-2.187	3.744

Table 16: Regression analysis adjusted Flesch score English

Table 15 and 16 contain the multiple regression analyses for the adjusted Flesch scores. The analyses consist of six independent variables each. The R Square values in both tables indicate that the analyses should not be interpreted as a conclusive model that considers all relevant factors.

Regression Statistics	
Multiple R	0.271
R Square	0.073
Adjusted R Sq.	0.016
Standard Error	9.666
Observations	104

ANOVA

	Degrees of Freedom	*Square Sums (SS)*	*Mean Square Sum (MS)*	*F*	*Significance F*
Regression	6	718.625	119.771	1.282	0.273
Residue	97	9062.555	93.428		
Total	103	9781.180			

	Coefficients	*Standard Error*	*t Stat*	*P-value*	*Lower 95%*	*Upper 95%*
Intercept	21.486	7.319	2.935	0.004	6.959	36.013
log Employees	-0.118	0.676	-0.174	0.862	-1.459	1.223
log Total Assets	0.008	0.695	0.012	0.991	-1.372	1.388
BvDEP Independence Indicator	1.163	0.888	1.310	0.193	-0.599	2.926
Share Price Volatility	0.652	3.482	0.187	0.852	-6.257	7.562
Profit Margin Increase	4.204	1.989	2.114	0.037	0.257	8.151
Revenue Increase	3.025	2.056	1.471	0.144	-1.056	7.107

Table 17: Regression analysis raw Flesch score German

Regression Statistics	
Multiple R	0.184
R Square	0.034
Adjusted R Sq.	-0.026
Standard Error	8.165
Observations	104

ANOVA

	Degrees of Freedom	*Square Sums (SS)*	*Mean Square Sum (MS)*	*F*	*Significance F*
Regression	6	227.253	37.875	0.568	0.755
Residue	97	6466.632	66.666		
Total	103	6693.885			

	Coefficients	*Standard Error*	*t Stat*	*P-value*	*Lower 95%*	*Upper 95%*
Intercept	45.866	6.183	7.418	0.000	33.594	58.137
log Employees	0.220	0.571	0.386	0.700	-0.912	1.353
log Total Assets	-0.114	0.587	-0.194	0.847	-1.279	1.052
BvDEP Independence Indicator	0.253	0.750	0.337	0.737	-1.236	1.742
Share Price Volatility	-0.074	2.941	-0.025	0.980	-5.910	5.763
Profit Margin Increase	1.927	1.680	1.147	0.254	-1.407	5.261
Revenue Increase	2.250	1.737	1.295	0.198	-1.197	5.698

Table 18: Regression analysis raw Flesch score English

Table 17 and 18 contain the multiple regression analyses for the raw Flesch scores. The low R Square values of the tables indicate that no conclusive model is found.

6.2.5 Testing Hypothesis 4 – Shareholder Independence

The influence of independence of managers from the shareholder on readability is evaluated with the BvDEP Independence Indicator that is transformed into dummy variables.

Although all four regression analyses indicate a positive influence of shareholder independence on readability, none does so at a significant level.

Hypothesis 4 is therefore **rejected.**

6.2.6 Testing Hypothesis 5 – Share Price Volatility

The volatility of the share price is calculated as the standard deviation of the year end prices between 2007 and 2011 divided by the average share price. This calculation accounts for the relativity of share price changes.

The regression analyses show no significant influence of share price volatility on readability in either direction.

Hypothesis 5 is therefore **rejected.**

6.2.7 Testing Hypothesis 6 – Financial Performance

6.2.7.1 Testing Hypothesis 6.1

The financial performance of a company is firstly measured as a function of the increase or decrease of the profit margin between 2008 and 2009. The dummy variable "1" indicates an increase, whereas "0" indicates a decrease of the profit margin.

A significant positive influence of profit margin increase on readability at the 90% level can be observed for the adjusted German Flesch score. Keeping all other variables constant, a profit margin increase leads to an average Flesch score increase of three points. For the raw German Flesch scores the influence of profit margin increase has a coefficient of 4.2 and is significant at the 95% level. Overall, one can truly speak of a significant relationship for the German scores.

The English letters to the shareholders are not significantly influenced by an increase of the profit margin.

Hypothesis 6.1 is therefore **partly accepted.**

Hypothesis 6.1 is **accepted for German** letters to the shareholders.

Hypothesis 6.1 is **rejected for English** letters to the shareholders.

6.2.7.2 Testing Hypothesis 6.2

Financial performance is secondly quantified as an increase or decrease of revenue between 2008 and 2009. The dummy variable "1" indicates an increase, whereas "0" indicates a decrease of revenues.

For the adjusted Flesch scores no significant influence of revenue increase can be found. However, there is a stronger tendency of relationship for the raw Flesch scores. The influence of revenue increase on the raw German Flesch score is significant at the 85% level, whereas for the raw English Flesch score it is significant at the 80% level. For a company that has increased its annual revenues, the average magnitude of readability increase is more than two points on the Flesch scale. Nevertheless, this result is still unconvincing due to its low significance level and the defined subordination of the results based on the raw scores in comparison to the adjusted scores.

Hypothesis 6.2 is therefore rejected.

6.2.8 Summary Table of Hypotheses Testing

This chapter aims to summarize the findings of the present chapter in a table.

	Hypothesis	Result
1.1	The readability of letters to the shareholders of quarterly reports is at a level that is commonly considered to be at least "difficult".	accepted for English, unanswered for German
1.1	The readability of letters to the shareholders of quarterly reports varies between different industries.	rejected
2	In bilingual reports, there is a linear correlation between the readability levels in German and English.	accepted
3	The readability of letters to the shareholders of quarterly reports is not dependent on company size.	accepted
4	The readability of letters to the shareholders in quarterly reports depends on the independence of the management from the shareholders.	rejected
5	The readability of letters to the shareholders in quarterly reports depends on share price volatility.	rejected
6.1	The readability of letters to the shareholders in quarterly reports depends on profit margins.	accepted for German, rejected for English
6.2	The readability of letters to the shareholders in quarterly reports depends on revenues.	rejected

Table 19: Summary of hypotheses testing

6.3 Discussion

The results of the conducted analyses contribute to existing research in various ways. On the one hand, previous studies can be, partially, confirmed. On the other hand, new insights into the topic of applied readability research in business reporting can be gained. Still, they are also subject to a variety of limitations that are discussed in chapter 6.4.

The findings on the level of readability of letters to the shareholders in reports confirm previous research.[215] With average Flesch scores of 43.24 for English reports and 21.72 for German reports, it has to be seriously questioned if the underlying reports are really open to the public. Additionally, since it seems plausible that the letters to the shareholders are among the most readable parts in a company report, the overall readability of the reports can be expected to be even lower and thus the reports seem to be reserved for the elite of society only. The obtained average Flesch values and some readable outliers clearly show that there is much room for improvement. Also in the light of staff participation programs it should be desirable that the provided information is being disclosed in an uncoded way. Future research could work on incentive systems or guidelines for companies to provide reports which are easier to read.

No difference of readability between industries can be found in this study. This is in line with the findings of *Courtis*.[216] On the one hand, this could be attributed to the fact that the vocabulary in letters to the shareholders is not as industry-specific as expected; on the other hand, existing differences could also outweigh each other. Most of all, the sample is split up which reduces explanatory power dramatically. This fact urgently has to be considered as a potential reason for the present results.

The finding that the readabilities of German and English reports correlate linearly at R^2=0.551 is entirely new. It offers an opportunity for future research to transfer results between languages to a limited extent. The correlation shows that if a company writes in a readable way in one language, the same can be expected for other languages as well. This interpretation also has implications for the intentionality of a certain reading ease. It appears that it is rather the product of a deliberate decision than a random one.

The influence of company size on readability is tested based on the natural logarithms of both the number of employees and the amount of the total assets. The inexistence of a significant relation is not in line with some trends in existing research.[217] The results of this study rather confirm the findings of *Courtis* and *Li*.[218] It seems that the term "company size" is

---

[215] cf. chapters 4.4.2 and 4.4.3
[216] Courtis (1995), p.10.
[217] Baker and Kare (1992), pp.2.
[218] Courtis (1995), pp.9. and Li (2008), pp.230.

insufficiently described by just one or two variables. Further research based on longitudinal studies of a broad range of companies could provide more insight into this topic.

Independence of managers from shareholders is found to have no significant influence on readability. This could result from the situation that existing governance mechanisms work the same way irrespective of the actual shareholder structure. It also cannot be excluded that the used variables only provide a limited impression of shareholder influence.

Share price volatility also is not found to have an influence on readability. This result is not in line with the findings of *Li*.[219] Though the used variables differ slightly in their practical implementation, it is surprising to observe such severe differences. Volatility, as it is used in this study, does not differentiate between pure upward swings, downward swings or varying price developments. Therefore, future research should not set the focus on *whether* share prices have been volatile, but *how* they have developed. The disparity to previous studies could be attributed to the different samples and the varying importance of capital markets for the firms. In Europe capital markets traditionally play a subordinate role in comparison to the influence of banks.

The influence of profit margin development on readability is surprisingly versatile. Only for the German letters to the shareholders a significant relation can be observed. This result mirrors the variety of different results in previous research.[220] On the basis of the underlying findings, a conclusive, general statement on the existence of management obfuscation cannot be provided. Still, the question why readability in German letters is significantly influenced by a profit margin change, while the readability in English is not, deserves future research. A potential reason could be that most companies of the sample are not located in countries where English is the main language. Therefore, assuming that the letters are written by non-natives, the linguistic flexibility to intentionally obscure information may be limited. Also for revenue increase the influence seems to be complex and opaque. Only a slight influence on the raw Flesch score of both languages can be observed. In general, both profit margin and revenue increase tend to have a more significant influence on the raw scores than on the adjusted scores. This result is by all means controversial since previous studies have never mentioned the issue of superfluous dots. It cannot be excluded that automated processing led to over-significant results.

The multiple regression analysis in this study must not, under any circumstances, be misinterpreted as a final model that allows predicting the readability of a letter to the

---

[219] Li (2008), pp.231.

[220] cf. chapter 4.4.3

shareholders, if the mentioned independent variables are available. Also the various limitations have to be considered.

In general, it appears that there is a broad mix of other factors that have influence on the readability of letters to the shareholders. Still, it seems obvious that the style of the writer(s) has a major influence on the readability. Future studies could try to find out certain writers' characteristics like age, education and background that have an influence and compare readability longitudinally when writers have changed within a company.

6.4 Limitations

This chapter is intended to specifically mention and discuss the limitations that have to be considered in the context of this study. Aiming to provide a point of reference for upcoming research, this section is kept deliberately self-critical to induce future improvements.

To begin with, the sample of the present study consists of the third quarter reports of 104 companies. This size is moderate which makes it possible to draw conclusions in the regression analyses. Compared to similar studies, the size is average. Nevertheless, for analyzing the difference in readability among industries, the acceptance limit for the minimum size of a subsample is reached. Moreover, the sample consists of quarterly reports listed on the FSE. This fact is deliberate and offers new insights. Nevertheless, comparisons with previous research undergo limitations and face difficulties. For the development of the hypotheses and interpretation of the results, the differences between previous samples and the present sample have to be neglected to a certain degree. The question how determinative the results for third quarter reports are in respect to other quarterly reports remains unanswered.

The general limitations and disadvantages of readability formulas have already been extensively discussed.[221] They are certainly severe, but located at an acceptable level, if the formulas are applied with care. Still, it has to be questioned whether the concepts are able to capture the same level of understandability as that felt by the reader. Besides, the present study uses the traditional Flesch formula to assess the readability of German texts. This application offers the advantage to compare two scores of one company. Nevertheless, a qualitative interpretation of German results is only possible to a certain extent. The decision to adjust the superfluous dots in letters to the shareholder is rigorous but necessary to arrive at more accurate readability scores.

The independent variables also have to be seen critically to some extent. As already mentioned, company size can only be inadequately described by the number of employees and the amount of the total assets. Moreover, the transformation of the values with the natural

---

[221] cf. chapter 4.3

logarithm is based on non-linear assumptions. The BvDEP Independence Indicator is already a severe simplification by itself. Further transformation into dummy variables (1 to 4), as applied in this study, makes it even more vulnerable to conceptual failures. A more fine-grained concept would increase accuracy of future studies. Moreover, the fact that the obtained BvDEP Independence Indicators are not from 2009 is problematic. Company's share price volatility is simplistically calculated based on five year-end snapshots of their respective share prices. Nevertheless, the main price trends should still be visible. The fact that not all share prices were available due to later issue of shares represents a minor limitation that can be accepted. A pure increase or decrease in profit margin or revenue does not per se mean that a company has performed better or worse. This also depends on the interpretation of managers and (potential) shareholders and could be seen in a competitive context as well.

The fact that the data is influenced by the recent global financial crisis could also have an impact on the generalizability of the results and their interpretation. A bias cannot be excluded.

In general, the small R Square values in the multiple regression analyses indicate that only a small fraction of independent variables has been tested in this study. A comprehensive model of what influences readability is not found. It has to be feared that other factors are difficult to measure empirically.

7. Conclusio

The present study aims to shed light on the issue of what influences the readability of letters to the shareholders of quarterly reports on the Frankfurt Stock Exchange with special regard to already existing literature in related fields.

Although it is prima facie quite conceivable that readability is simply the product of the writer's style, certain capital market theories suggest that managers have an incentive to actively control and adjust the readability for their purpose. By obfuscating, managers can influence capital market reactions to their personal advantage. Various studies have shown a relation between company performance and readability. Still, an equal amount has shown that this is not the case. Moreover, there is discord whether factors like company size, industry sector or shareholder influence affect reading ease.

This study confirms the discord in previous literature. There are tendencies towards obfuscation in German letters to the shareholders, but not in their English pendants. The other mentioned factors seem to have no significant influence on readability.

Based on this study it can be argued that potential factors which have an influence on readability of company narratives have not yet been hypothesized and discovered. Future research needs to set a special focus on soft factors that are difficult to measure.

Nevertheless, the topic of readability research has finally involved German companies and their quarterly reports. It remains to be hoped that scholars extend research in this particular area and provide more insights. The practical impact and potential pressure on companies that can be created by such studies should not be underestimated. Investors have a right to receive clear and honest information in return for their capital.

References and Sources

Adelberg, A. (1979): A methodology for measuring the understandability of financial report messages. Journal of Accounting Research, 17(2): 565-592

Abrahamson, E. / Amir, E. (1996): The information content of the president's letter to shareholders. Journal of Business Finance and Accounting, 23(8): 1157-1182

Andriof, J. / Waddock, S. / Husted, B. / Rahman, S. (2002): Unfolding Stakeholder Thinking: Theory, Responsibility and Engagement. Sheffield, Greenleaf: 1. Ed.

Baker, H. / Kare, D. (1992): Relationship Between Annual Report Readability and Corporate Financial Performance. Management Research News, 15(1): 1-4

Balata, P. / Breton, G. (2005): Narratives vs Numbers in the Annual Report: Are They Giving the Same Message to the Investors? Review of Accounting and Finance, 4(2): 5-14

Barnett, A. / Leoffler, K. (1979): Readability of accounting and auditing messages. Journal of Business Communication, 16(3): 49–59

Bickley, A. / Ellington, B. / Bickley, R. (1970): The Cloze Procedure: A Conspectus. Journal of Literacy Research, 2: 232-249

Bloomfield, R. (2002): The "Incomplete Revelation Hypothesis" and Financial Reporting. Accounting Horizons, 16(3): 233-243

Bloomfiled, R. (2008): Discussion of ''Annual report readability, current earnings, and earnings persistence''. Journal of Accounting and Economics, 45: 248-252

Börsenordnung für die Frankfurter Wertpapierbörse (2013): (http://deutsche-boerse.com/dbg/dispatch/de/binary/dbg_nav/metanavigation/30_Regulations?object_id=84XHGZ360NSGDDE, downloaded on 11.02.2013)

Brown, J. / Forster, W. (2013): CSR and Stakeholder Theory: A Tale of Adam Smith. Journal of Business Ethics, 112(2): 301-312

Bruce, B. / Rubin, A. / Starr, K. (1981): Why readability formulas fail. IEEE Transactions on Professional Communication, 24(1): 50-52

Bureau van Dijk (2008): BvDEP Ownership Database, (http://biblioteca.cchs.csic.es/docs/formacion/GuiaAccionariado.pdf, downloaded on 20.02.2013)

Clarkson, M. (1995): A Stakeholder Framework for Analyzing and Evaluating Corporate Social Performance. Academy of Management Review, 20(1): 92-117

Cornell, B. / Shapiro, A. (1987): Corporate Stakeholders and Corporate Finance. Financial Management, 16: 5-14

Courtis, J. (1995): Readability of annual reports: Western versus Asian evidence. Accounting, Auditing & Accountability Journal. 8(2): 4-17

Courtis, J. (1986): An Investigation into Annual Report Readability and Corporate Risk-Return Relationships. Accounting and Business Research, Autumn: 285-294

Courtis, K. (1998): Annual report readability variability: tests of the obfuscation hypothesis. Accounting, Auditing & Accountability Journal, 11(4): 459-471

Courtis, K. (2004): Corporate report obfuscation: artifact or phenomenon? The British Accounting Review, 36: 291-312

Crossley, S. / Allen, B. / McNamara, D. (2011): Text readability and intuitive simplification: A comparison of readability formulas, Reading in a Foreign Language, 23(1): 84-101

Crossley, S. / Dufty, D. / McCarthy, P. / McNamara, D. (2007): Toward a new readability: A mixed model approach. In McNamara and Trafton (Eds.), Proceedings of the 29th annual conference of the Cognitive Science Society (197–202). Austin, TX: Cognitive Science Society

Dale, E. / Chall, J. (1948): A formula for predicting readability. Educational Research Bulletin, 27: 11-54

Dale, E. / Chall, J. (1949): The concept of readability. Elementary English, 26: 19-26

Dempsey, S. / Harrison, D. / Luchtenberg, K. / Seiler, M. (2012): Financial Opacity and Firm Performance: The Readability of REIT Annual Reports. The Journal of Real Estate Finance and Economics, 45(2): 450-470

Deutsche Euroshop AG (2009): Report 3rd Quarter, (http://files.shareholder.com/downloads/NFLX/1028772132x0x364065/2add3064-3eea-4266-80c3-c6090d4bafc1/Netflix_-_2009_Annual_Report.pdf, downloaded on 02.03.2013)

Downes, J. / Goodman, J. (2003): Finance & Investment Handbook. New York, Barron's: 6. Ed.

Dreyer, L. (1984): Readability and responsibility. Journal of Reading, 27: 334-339

DuBay, W. (2006): The Classic Readability Studies, Costa Mesa: Impact Information

Eisenhardt, K. (1989): Agency Theory: An Assessment and Review. Academy of Management Review, 14(1): 57-74

Elliot, B. / Elliot, J. (2006): Financial Accounting, Reporting and Analysis: International Edition. Harlow, Pearson: 2. Ed.

Fama, E. (1970): Efficient capital markets: A review of theory and empirical work. Journal of Finance, 25(2): 282-417

Figge, F. / Schalteger, S. (2000): Was ist "Stakeholder Value"? Vom Schlagwort zur Messung, (http://www2.leuphana.de/umanagement/csm/content/nama/downloads/download_publikationen/02-3downloadversion.pdf, downloaded on 13.02.2013)

Flesch, R. (1948): A New Readability Yardstick. Journal of Applied Psychology, 32(3): 221-233

Freeman, E. (1984): Strategic Management: A stakeholder approach. Boston: Pitman

Freeman, E. (1999): Divergent Stakeholder Theory. Academy of Management Review, 24(2): 233-236

Freeman, E. / Reed, E. (1983): Stockholders and Shareholders: A new perspective on Corporate Governance. California Management Review, 25(3): 88-106

Graesser, A. / McNamara, D. / Louwerse, M. / Cai, Z. (2004): Coh-Metrix: Analysis of text on cohesion and language. Behavioral Research Methods, Instruments, and Computers, 36(2): 193–202

Gunning, R. (1969): The Fog Index after twenty years. Journal of Business Communication, 6(2): 3-13

Heiden, M. (2006): Pro-forma-Berichterstattung: Reporting zwischen Information und Täuschung. Berlin, Erich Schmidt Verlag: 1. Aufl.

Heun, M. (2007): Finanzmarktsimulation mit Multiagentensystemen. Wiesbaden, Gabler: 1. Aufl.

Hooghiemstra, R. (2010): Letters to the shareholders: A content analysis comparison of letters written by CEOs in the U.S. and Japan, 1-52, (http://business.illinois.edu/accountancy/research/vkzcenter/conferences/italy/papers/Hooghiemstra.pdf, downloaded on 23.01.2013)

Hossain, M. / Siddiquee, M. (2008): Readability of Management Reviews of Listed Companies of Bangladesh, Working Paper, http://papers.ssrn.com/sol3/papers.cfm?abstract_id=1079695, downloaded on 09.01.2013

Jensen, M. / Meckling, W. (1976): Theory of the Firm: Managerial Behavior, Agency Costs and Ownership Structure. Journal of Financial Economics, 3 (4): 305-360

Jones, M. (1994): A Comment to Contextualize "Performance and Readability: A Comparison of Annual Reports of Profitable and Unprofitable Corporations". Journal of Business Communication, 31(3): 225-230

Jones, M. (1988): A longitudinal study of the readability of the chairman's narratives in the corporate reports of a UK company. Accounting and Business Research, 18(72): 297-305

Jordan, R. (1973): An Empirical Investigation of the Adjustments of Stock Prices to New Quarterly Earnings Information. Journal of Financial & Quantitative Analysis, 8(4): 609-620

Korn, J. (1997): Schwankungsreserven im handelsrechtlichen Jahresabschluß von Schaden- und Unfallversicherungsunternehmen. Karlsruhe, Verlag Versicherungswirtschaft e.V.: 1. Aufl.

KPMG (2013): Quartalsfinanzbericht (http://www.kpmg.de/Themen/1866.htm, downloaded on 11.02.2013)

Lehavy, R. / Li, F. / Merkley, K. (2011): The Effect of Annual Report Readability on Analyst Following and the Properties of Their Earnings Forecasts. The Accounting Review, 86(3): 1087-1115

Leichtlesbar.ch (2013): Warum verwenden Sie die englische statt der deutschen Formel? (http://www.leichtlesbar.ch/html/faq+78.html, viewed on 16.12.2013)

Lewis, N. / Parker, L. / Pound, G. / Sutcliffe, P. (1986): Accounting Report Readability: The Use of Readability Techniques. Accounting and Business Research, 16(63): 199-213

Li, F. (2008): Annual report readability, current earnings, and earnings persistence. Journal of Accounting and Economics, 45: 221-247

Malkiel, B. (2003): The Efficient Market Hypothesis and Its Critics. Journal of Economic Perspectives, 17(1): 59-82

McConnell, D. / Haslem, J. / Gibson, V. (1986): The president's letter to the stockholders: a new look. Financial Analysts Journal, 42(5): 66-70

Miles, S. (2012): Stakeholder: Essentially Contested or Just Confused? Journal of Business Ethics, 108(3): 285-298

Mohamad, R. / Rahman, A. (2006): Readability of Corporate Annual Reports of Top 200 Malaysian Companies, 10(1): 33-47

Netflix, Inc. (2009): Annual Report, (http://files.shareholder.com/downloads/NFLX/1028772132x0x364065/2add3064-3eea-4266-80c3-c6090d4bafc1/Netflix_-_2009_Annual_Report.pdf, downloaded on 24.01.2013)

Oakland, T. / Lane, H. (2004): Language, reading, and readability formulas: Implications for developing and adapting test. International Journal of Testing, 4(3): 239-252

Parmar, B. / Freeman, E. / Harrison, J. / Wicks, A. / Purnell, L. / De Colle, S. (2010): Stakeholder Theory: The State of the Art. The Academy of Management Journal, 4(19): 403-445

Pashalian, S. / Crissy, W. (1950): How Readable Are Corporate Annual Reports? Journal of Applied Psychology, 34(4): 244-248

Post, J. / Preston, L. / Sachs, S. (2002): Redefining the Corporation: Stakeholder Management and Organizational Wealth. Stanford, Stanford University Press: 1. Ed.

Readability-Score.com (2013): Free Online Readability Calculator (www.readability-score.com, opened on between 02.01.2013 and 03.03.2013)

Redish, J. (2000): Readability Formulas Have Even More Limitations Than Klare Discusses. ACM Journal of Computer Documentation, 24(3): 132-137

Redish, J. / Selzer, J. (1985): The place of readability formulas in technical communication. Technical Communication, 32(4): 46-52

Ross (1973): The Economic Theory of Agency: The Principal's Problem. The American Economic Review, 63(2): 134-139.

Rutherford, B. (2003): Obfuscation, textual complexity and the role of regulated narrative accounting disclosure in corporate governance. Journal of Management and Governance, 7(2): 187-210

Scheufele, B. / Haas, A. (2008): Medien und Aktien: Theoretische und empirische Modelling der Rolle der Berichterstattung für das Börsengeschehen. Wiesbaden, VS Verlag: 1. Aufl.

Shleifer, A. (2000): Inefficient Markets: An Introduction to Behavioral Finance. New York, Oxford University Press: 1. Ed.

Smith, M. / Jamil, A. / Johari, Y. / Ahmad, S. (2006): The Chairman's Statement in Malaysian Companies: A Test of the Obfuscation Hypothesis. Asian Review of Accounting, 14(1/2): 49-65

Smith, M. / Taffler, R. (1992): Readability and Understandability: Different Measures of the Textual Complexity of Accounting Narrative. Accounting, Auditing & Accountability Journal, 5(4): 84-98

Smith, M. / Taffler, R. (2000): The chairman's statement - A content analysis of discretionary narrative disclosures. Accounting, Auditing & Accountability Journal, 13(5): 624-647

Soper, F. / Dolphin, R. (1964): Readability and corporate annual reports. The Accounting Review, 39: 358-362

Stittle, J. (2003): Annual Reports: Delivering Your Corporate Message to Your Stakeholders. Hampshire, Gower: 1. Ed.

Stolowy, H. / Lebas, M. (2006): Financial Accounting and Reporting – A Global Perspective. London, Cengage: 2. Ed.

Strieder, T. (2003): Jahresabschlusskompetenz. Berlin, Erich Schmidt: 1. Aufl.

Subramanian, R. / Insley, R. / Blackwell, R. (1993): Performance and Readability: A Comparison of Annual Reports of Profitable and Unprofitable Corporations. The Journal of Business Communication, 30(1): 49-61

Taylor, W. (1953): Cloze Procedure: A Tool for Measuring Readability. Journalism Quarterly, 30(4): 415-433

Tekfi, C. (1987): Readability formulas: An overview. Journal of Documentation, 43(3): 261-273

The Heights (2013): Letter to the Shareholders, Online guide, (http://theheights-planning.com/pdf/Letter%20To%20Shareholders.pdf, downloaded on 24.01.2013)

Website Frankfurter Wertpapierbörse (2013): Wissen rund um die Börse, (http://www.boerse-frankfurt.de/de/wissen#reiter=boersefrankfurt, sub links, downloaded on 07.02.2013)

Wentges, P. (2002): Corporate Governance und Stakeholder-Ansatz: Implikationen für die betriebliche Finanzwirtschaft. Wiesbaden, Gabler: 1. Aufl.

WpHG (2013): Gesetze über den Wertpapierhandel (http://www.gesetze-im-internet.de/wphg/, downloaded on 11.02.2013)

WU Library (2013): Orbis, (http://www.wu.ac.at/library/search/databases/info/orbis, viewed between 15.12.2012 and 27.02.2013)